List of resources on the CD-ROM

The page numbers refer to the teacher's notes provided in this book.

Photographs: © 2007, Peter Rowe; © 2008, Kate Pedlar; Lamps image © 2007, Next plc (www.next.co.uk)

INTRODUCTION

This book and CD-ROM support the teaching and learning of a selection of units from the QCA Scheme of Work for design and technology at Key Stage 2. Some of the more successful and popular units from the QCA scheme have been kept while fresh themes and ideas have been developed for teachers who would like to move their scheme of work forward; units now include links to ICT and 'Photograph frames' also allows a discussion on sustainability. Some topics have been adapted: 'Money containers', for example, has been become the topic 'Bags'. The full range of skills and knowledge across the design and technology subject area are covered within the five chapters included here (food, textiles, structures and systems) with a clear progression of skills in all areas through each of the three books in this series.

The activities in every chapter lead the teacher through all the necessary elements of a design and technology project, ensuring that it is well structured, comprising of a design and making assignment, focused practical tasks to develop skills and investigative activities to evaluate existing products. In each chapter children are encouraged to focus on the user and purpose as well as the function and aesthetics, creating a final product that fulfils specific criteria that they themselves set at the beginning of the project. In addition, children are introduced to designing strategies that will lead them to more creative and innovative ideas for their projects. Additional support and resources (such as ideas for investigations, video clips or step-by-step guidance on how to make items) have been provided for those QCA units that have been seen as difficult or more technical to teach.

Resources on the CD-ROM
All the images, sound and video clips on the CD-ROM have been specifically chosen to support the teaching of these units and broaden the areas of study. They include photographs, for example of different types of bag, photograph frames and salad ingredients, and film clips showing ways to cut fruit and vegetables, how to sew using a variety of stitches and different types of lever in action.

Photocopiable pages
The worksheets in the book accompany the children's investigations, focused practical tasks and design and make activities. They can be used to build a process diary for each unit, which should be supplemented with any other sketches, photographs and written work the children create as part of the project.

Word cards and glossaries
The vocabulary of design and technology is often new to the children and therefore there are word cards and glossaries provided on the CD-ROM where necessary. These can be used as worksheets to be read through with the children or the cards can be used to label display materials.

Health and safety
Notes on health and safety are provided in the introduction to each unit, and photocopiable sheets are provided on the CD-ROM illustrating safe usage of equipment, such as hand drills and hacksaws. Always use any advice in this book and CD-ROM in conjunction with your own school policy.

Contexts
Outcomes in design and technology are usually more successful when the children understand why they are undertaking a particular project. They need to be clear about the problem or need, the person or people affected by this need and the resources available to realise solutions to that need. Although some suggestions for final products are made, such as making a night light for a child's bedroom in 'Lighting it up', these should be considered carefully when setting the task: the context will influence the direction that the children's ideas take.

HOW TO USE THE CD-ROM

Windows NT® users
If you use Windows NT® you may see the following error message: 'The procedure entry point Process32First could not be located in the dynamic link library KERNEL32.dll'. Click on **OK** and the CD-ROM will autorun with no further problems.

Windows Vista™ users
If you use Windows Vista™ you may see the following error message: Click on **OK** and the CD will autorun automatically.

Resources on this CD-ROM can be viewed using an interactive whiteboard, data projector or PC.

Setting up your computer for optimal use
On opening, the CD-ROM will alert you if changes are needed in order to operate the CD-ROM at its optimal use.

To see images at their maximum screen size, your screen display needs to be set to 800 x 600 pixels. In order to adjust your screen you will need to **Quit** the program.

If using a PC, open the **Control Panel**. Select **Display** and then **Settings**. Adjust the **Desktop Area** to 800 x 600 pixels. Click on **OK** and then restart the program.

If using a Mac, select **Displays** under **System Preferences** and choose 800 x 600 screen size from the list of options.

To print PDF versions of the images and to view and print the photocopiable pages you need Adobe® Acrobat® Reader® installed on your computer. This can be downloaded from www.acrobatdownload-ib.com.

To view videos on your computer you need QuickTime™ installed on your computer. This can be downloaded from www.apple.com/quicktime/download.

Menu screen
▶ Click on the **Resource Gallery** of your choice to review the resources available under that theme.
▶ Click on **Complete Resource Gallery** to view all the images, videos and audio files available on the CD.
▶ Click on **Photocopiable Resources** to view and print the photocopiable resources also provided in the book that accompanies this CD-ROM.
▶ Click **Back** to return to the opening screen.
▶ Click **Quit** to exit the program.

Resource Galleries
▶ Click **Help** to find support on accessing and using images.
▶ Click **Back** to return to the **Menu**.
▶ Click **Quit** to exit the program.

Viewing images
Small versions of each image are shown in the Resource Galleries. Click and drag the slide bar to scroll through the images in the gallery, or click on the arrows to move the images frame by frame.
▶ Click on an image to view the screen-size version of it.
▶ To return to the gallery click **Back to Resource Gallery**.

Viewing videos
Click on the video icon of your choice in the Resource Gallery. In order to view the videos on this CD-ROM you will need to have QuickTime™ installed on your computer (see 'Setting up your computer for optimal use' above).

Once at the video screen, use the buttons on the bottom of the video screen to operate the video. The slide bar can be used for fast forward and rewind. To return to the Resource Gallery click on **Back to Resource Gallery**.

If you encounter any problems when viewing footage, check that your computer fulfils the minimum specifications (see page 2). If there are still problems running the footage, try using a different version of QuickTime™ (such as 7.13.1).

Listening to sound recordings

Click on the required sound icon. Use the buttons or the slide bar to hear the sound. A transcript will be played in a viewing window where appropriate. To return to the gallery, click **Back to Resource Gallery**.

Printing

Click on the image to view it (see 'Viewing images' above). There are two print options.

Print using Acrobat enables you to print a large copy of the image as a PDF file. These are often a higher quality than printing images from the screen. Once you have printed the resource, minimise or close the Adobe® screen using – or X in the top right-hand corner of the screen. To return to the Resource Gallery, click on **Back to Resource Gallery**.

Simple print enables you to print the image without the need to use **Adobe® Acrobat® Reader®**. Select the image and click on the **Simple print** option. After printing, click on **Back to Resource Gallery**.

Slideshow presentation

If you would like to present a number of resources without having to return to the Resource Gallery, you can create a slideshow.

In the gallery, click on the + tabs at the top of each image you would like to use. It is important that you click on the images in order; a number will appear on each tab to confirm the order. If you would like to change the order, click on **Clear slideshow** and start again.

Once you have selected your images – up to a maximum of 20 – click on **Play slideshow**.

To move between slides on your slideshow, click on the blue arrows either side of the screen.

You can end your slideshow presentation at any time by clicking on **Back to Resource Gallery**. Your slideshow selection will remain selected until you **Clear slideshow** or return to the **Menu screen**.

Photocopiable resources

To view or print a photocopiable resource page, click on the required title on the list and the page will open as a read-only page in **Adobe® Acrobat®**. In order to access these files you will need **Adobe® Acrobat® Reader®** installed on your computer.

To print the selected resource, select **File** and then **Print**. Once you have printed the resource, minimise or close the Adobe screen. This will take you back to the list of PDF files. To return to the **Menu**, click on **Back**.

Using this CD-ROM with other programs

To switch between this CD-ROM and other programs on your computer, hold down the 'alt' key on your keyboard and then press 'tab'.

Technical support

For all technical support queries, please phone Scholastic Customer Services on 0845 603 9091.

HEALTHIER LUNCH BOXES

Content and skills

This chapter links to Unit 3B 'Sandwich snacks' of the QCA Scheme of Work for design and technology at Key Stage 2. It broadens the focus of the QCA unit by allowing children to look at interesting salads and samosas rather than sandwiches. The Healthier lunch boxes resource gallery on the CD-ROM, together with the teacher's notes and photocopiable pages in this chapter, can be used to support the teaching of this QCA unit.

Throughout the chapter, children are introduced to a range of different foods that could be part of their lunch box. They will identify and sort ingredients into the eatwell-plate food groups and they will explore foods by tasting, finding out what ingredients they contain, looking at how they are made and what they are called. They will be able to use ingredients in different combinations and there are opportunities to investigate and evaluate different products and to use appropriate vocabulary to describe them.

The chapter is structured as follows:

▶ Investigating fruit and vegetables.
▶ Tasting fruit and vegetables.
▶ Investigating other salad ingredients.
▶ Making a salad.
▶ Exploring salad dressings and toppings.
▶ Exploring combinations of ingredients.
▶ Making vegetable samosas.
▶ Design and make activity.
▶ Evaluating their salads or samosas.

Photograph © 2007, Peter Rowe

Outcome

The main outcome of this unit will be for children to design and make a salad or other item suitable for their lunch box. In doing this, the children will be expected to:

▶ evaluate a range of lunch-box items
▶ investigate a range of ingredients
▶ use information from the evaluation and investigation activities to select and prepare a healthy lunch-box item
▶ suggest a range of lunch-box items, evaluate them against their criteria for making and consider the eatwell-plate food groups
▶ combine a range of ingredients to create an appealing lunch-box item
▶ consider how well their food item meets the original purpose
▶ have an understanding of the 'balanced plate' model for healthy eating and apply this understanding to ideas about how the food item contributes to a healthy diet.

Health and safety

When working with food, it is important to demonstrate accurate, effective and appropriate use of equipment, using safe and hygienic working practices. Ensure that:

▶ Surfaces are cleaned with antibacterial cleaner
▶ A plastic table cover is kept for food activities and used to cover wooden/old tables
▶ Aprons are provided for food preparation
▶ There are appropriate storage facilities
▶ Food equipment is kept in a clearly labelled cupboard
▶ Safe practice is taught in relation to using equipment such as knives – refer to your school's health and safety policy.

Remember to obtain parental permission before tasting sessions to identify any allergies, cultural or dietary requirements. Children who are unable to eat certain types of food should be given alternatives.

Links to other subjects

Science: irreversible changes; skills such as discovering, sorting, sequencing.

Maths: calculating the cost of making a particular food product; changing the amounts of recipe ingredients to make it suitable for a greater number of people; research into favourite foods then representing findings in graphical form; links with mass, weight and capacity.

English: making collections of words related to foods and their sensory characteristics to help children evaluate food products; sentence-level work such as experimenting with adverbs when writing about their lunch-box food; text-level work such as writing recipes, analysing instructional texts, writing a non-chronological report about different snacks; using simple flowcharts to plan work.

Geography: identifying countries where different salads originate; finding out about salads traditionally associated with specific countries such as Italy and Greece.

ICT: using an interactive whiteboard and clipart to create designs; using a computer to create a bar chart or pictogram showing favourite foods; using a digital camera to record food processing skills; using desktop publishing software to produce recipes for food products; using the internet to find information about salads.

Organising the unit

All three types of activity should be undertaken (investigating and evaluating, focused practical tasks, designing and making). The order in which they are undertaken can be of the teacher's choosing. For example, starting points could be:

▶ setting the design and make activity
▶ investigating what different foods the children currently eat for lunch
▶ discussing healthy and unhealthy food.

Resources on the CD-ROM

The gallery of resources includes photographs of different types of foods that could be included in a lunch box such as samosas, soup, fruit and sandwiches. There are photographs that show collections of various ingredients that could be used as part of a salad to help children recognise different ingredients. Also included are ingredients that could be used in dressings and toppings for salads as well as the ingredients and equipment needed for making samosas. The eatwell-plate model is included as the standard way of teaching about food groups. In addition, there are videos to support the teaching of practical skills, including how to cut and grate vegetables safely.

Photocopiable pages

These include:

▶ sensory descriptors to use when describing fruit, vegetables and salad ingredients
▶ choosing ingredients for a salad, taking into consideration the eatwell-plate model
▶ a recipe, equipment and method for making vegetable samosas
▶ planning the design and make activity
▶ evaluating salads.

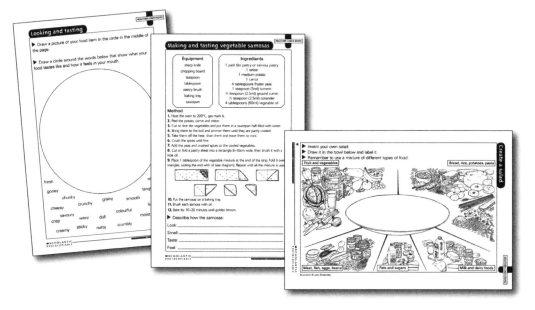

INVESTIGATING AND EVALUATING IDEAS

INVESTIGATING FRUIT AND VEGETABLES

Photographs: Salad ingredients 1, Salad ingredients 2, Salad ingredients 3

The photographs on the CD-ROM give the opportunity to show children the variety of fruits and vegetables that could be part of a salad. There are photographs of many kinds of fruits and vegetables, of carbohydrate foods that could be a part of a salad (couscous, potatoes, rice, pasta), different varieties of the same vegetable (cherry, sun-dried and vine tomatoes), ingredients that could be used for dressings and ingredients for use as toppings.

Discussing the photographs

▶ Look at 'Salad ingredients 1, 2 and 3' and ask if the children are able to name the different fruit and vegetables (1 shows lettuce, fresh tomatoes, sun-dried tomatoes, cucumber, peas and peppers; 2 shows pineapple, beetroot, sweetcorn, apple, olives, avocado, egg, radishes and spring onions; 3 shows pasta, potatoes, white rice, wild rice, kidney beans, chickpeas, pumpkin seeds and sunflower seeds). On the board, play 'Hangman' with the some of the letters included to help the children guess the name of the salad ingredient.

▶ Talk with the children about when they have eaten the different fruits and vegetables. Which ones do they eat at home? How often do they eat them? When have they eaten the different ingredients?

▶ Discuss with the children different ways in which they could sort the foods in the photographs according to their shape, colour, type of seed, whether they are grown underground, can be eaten without cooking, or should be peeled before use. Discuss what other foods could be added to the groups. If possible, complement the photographs with samples of some of the ingredients – from the school allotment or garden.

Photographs © 2007, Peter Rowe

TASTING FRUIT AND VEGETABLES

Illustration: World map

Photocopiable page: Looking and tasting   PAGES 15

There are so many different fruits and vegetables that it would be time-consuming and expensive to have several samples. It is sufficient to have two or three fruits and two or three vegetables that the children may not have seen before, would find exciting to look at, prepare and taste, and may be suitable eventually for the product they will prepare.

See your school's health and safety policy and the notes in the introduction to this unit for guidance on health and safety issues related to tasting sessions (for example, food allergies).

Discussion

▶ Discuss with the children what they think of when you say 'salad'. Ask them what ingredients they have seen in salad, what sort of salads they have eaten and the kinds of things they like and dislike about salads.

▶ Discuss one of the samples with the children. Model the process of describing the item for them. For example: 'This fruit is called a mango, its skin is smooth and it's a green/red colour. It feels quite firm and is an oval shape. Inside is a large stone the same shape as the fruit. The flesh is bright yellow and very juicy.' Ask questions about the food as this process is going on. Ask the children what they think the inside will look like and what colour they think it is. Do they think it will have pips or a stone? Ask whether it will it be hard or soft inside. Link the investigation to specific people or characters in storybooks to help children use their imagination. Which vegetable do they think Mr and Mrs Twit would like to eat and why?

▶ In a similar way, discuss and model how children should taste samples and record their findings. For example: 'This mango smells perfumed or fragrant. When I put it in my mouth it is very juicy and tastes sweet. It feels soft on my tongue and is easy to chew.' The remaining samples can be evaluated together or in smaller groups.

Activities

▶ The children should complete the 'Looking and tasting' photocopiable on page 15 using the different samples of fruit and vegetables. This activity involves drawing the fruit or vegetable and choosing from the words on the sheet to describe how it looks, feels and tastes.

▶ Show the children a selection of bought salads, for example, Greek salad, tabbouleh, Caesar salad and salads containing couscous, potato, noodles, pasta, rice. Ask the children to look at the salads and then identify and list the different ingredients. Ask them which ingredients they have tried and which they are not familiar with. Talk about the countries from which the salads originated – use the outline map of the world in the gallery to identify different countries or areas of the world.

INVESTIGATING OTHER SALAD INGREDIENTS

Photograph: The eatwell plate

Photocopiable pages: What's in the salad?, Evaluating salad ingredients   PAGES 16–17

Use the different salads as an opportunity for the children to learn about the eatwell plate and discuss how we need a balance of different types of food for a healthy diet. Have available a range of interesting ingredients from the four main groups in the eatwell-plate model (bread, other cereals and potatoes; fruit and vegetables; milk and dairy foods; meat, fish and alternatives) for a tasting session, for example; radish, olives, sun-dried tomatoes, dried fruit, a selection of canned pulses, seeds, cheeses, cooked rice/couscous/pasta.

Discussing the photograph

▶ Use the photograph to teach or revise the eatwell-plate model. Draw the children's attention to the size of the sections and what this means. Use one of the salads discussed previously, such as the Greek salad, and sort its components into the eatwell-plate groups. Discuss what food groups are included and what could be added to cover more of the food groups.

Activities

▶ Ask the children to divide the ingredients of other salads into the different groups of the eatwell plate, using the 'What's in the salad?' photocopiable on page 16. You may need to discuss the ingredients of various salads, or provide pictures from magazines, before the children start the worksheet.

▶ Discuss with the children the foods that have been brought into the classroom. They could record their thoughts on the 'Evaluating salad ingredients' photocopiable on page 17, which includes descriptive vocabulary for appearance, smell, taste and texture.

▶ Ask the children to think about the different ways in which salads form part of a meal (they can be a main meal or a side dish). Ask them to consider how the salads would differ for each occasion.

FOCUSED PRACTICAL TASKS

MAKING A SALAD

Videos: Cutting (bridge technique), Cutting (claw technique), Grating, Peeling

Photocopiable page: Create a salad   PAGE 18

This activity allows the children to see what they have discussed being put into practice. They learn how ingredients can be combined to make a salad as well as how to use equipment safely. The main activity will be to demonstrate how to make a salad of the teacher's choosing. Use the videos to show the correct techniques for cutting, grating and peeling, especially if the ingredients are prepared (peeled, chopped and grated) before the demonstration.

Discussing the videos

▶ Before demonstrating how to make a salad, show the 'Cutting', 'Grating' and 'Peeling' videos (depending on the type of salad you are making). Ask questions to reinforce the key points of the demonstrations and ensure that the children remember to: use the 'claw' or 'bridge' technique to stabilise the item they are cutting; take care with peelers; leave a small amount at the end of the item they are grating to avoid grating their fingers.

▶ Highlight the importance of good hygiene and point out the apron, plastic chopping board and clean hands and nails in the video demonstrations.

▶ Discuss how different effects can be achieved by cutting or grating vegetables in different ways. For example, grating items finely or chopping carrots into chunks, discs or batons.

Activities

▶ Show the children a variety of ways in which to put a salad together. Start with one of the foods from the 'Bread, other cereals and potatoes' group and add ingredients from other groups. Discuss what the children think the salad could look like at the end – mixed, layered, separate sections, and how it might be presented (in a bowl, on a plate, in a pitta pocket). Discuss what could be included to add colour – tomatoes, radishes, yellow pepper. Ask the children who the salad could be for – a vegetarian, a person with a food intolerance?

▶ Children could draw their ideas for salads for two or three people at this point using the 'Create a salad' photocopiable on page 18. Start them off with ideas by asking what type of salad the main character in their class book would eat. Ask the children to identify which section of the eatwell plate each ingredient comes from. What suggestions could they make to ensure the salad includes foods from a number of sections from the eatwell plate?

EXPLORING SALAD DRESSINGS AND TOPPINGS

Photographs: Salad dressings, Salad toppings

These tasks encourage the children to consider how salads can be made to look and taste different by adding dressings and toppings. Dressings to take to the classroom could include mayonnaise, salad cream, yogurt and mint dressing, French dressing, olive oil or lime juice. Toppings could be croutons (spread squares of bread with melted butter then sprinkle on herbs, salt, grated cheese, and bake in the oven for about 30 minutes, medium heat), different seeds (sesame, pumpkin, poppy, mixed), crispy onion bits, grilled bacon pieces, herbs and spices. All these toppings provide opportunities for the children to taste, evaluate and develop their ideas of what they would be a tasty topping.

Discussing the photographs

▶ Using 'Salad dressings', talk about the different types of dressing that the children already know. Discuss which items could be mixed together to create a dressing, such as the herbs and oil, pesto and mayonnaise or oil, vinegar and mustard.

▶ Using the 'Salad toppings' photograph, find out which toppings the children are familiar with already. Identify the different items (croutons, parmesan, bacon pieces, pumpkin seeds, sunflower seeds and pine nuts). Can the children think of any way to change the taste of any of these (for example, toasting the seeds)?

Activities

▶ Taste some of the dressings brought to the lesson using bread sticks or vegetable sticks. Which do the children prefer? Encourage them to suggest different dressings they have tried or would like to try. Introduce or use descriptive words with the children such as 'zesty', 'spicy', 'fruity', 'herby', 'minty' and encourage them to use them in a sentence to describe the dressings they have tried.

▶ Demonstrate how to make a dressing for the salad. For example, stir some pesto into mayonnaise, or mix balsamic vinegar, olive oil and a squeeze of lemon juice together. Dress a salad (some mixed leaves, for example) and discuss how the dressing has changed the appearance of the salad, and whether the children think it looks more appetising with or without this addition.

▶ Demonstrate how to create a topping for the salad. For example, sprinkle on some bacon pieces or sesame seeds. If possible, toast the seeds beforehand. Discuss how the topping has changed the appearance and texture of the salad and whether the children think it looks more appetising with or without this addition.

EXPLORING COMBINATIONS OF INGREDIENTS

Photographs: The eatwell plate

Photocopiable page: Looking and tasting **PAGE 15**

This focused practical task teaches/reinforces practical skills and will help children to think about colour combinations, textures and flavours for salads for future work. It also extends their knowledge about combining ingredients for successful outcomes.

Explain to the children that they are going to prepare and then add a different ingredient to one of the following salad bases: boiled rice, cooked couscous, potatoes or boiled pasta – so that they can see what different combinations look like and what they taste like. Refer to your school's health and safety policy for cooking and tasting food. If rice and pasta are to be cooked beforehand, cool them quickly after cooking, cover them and keep them in a fridge until it is time for them to be used. Do not reheat rice once it has been cooked.

Discussing the photographs

Use the 'Eatwell plate' photograph to show the children different types of carbohydrates/ starchy foods available (potatoes, noodles, couscous, boiled rice, cooked pasta). Highlight the fact that these foods all belong to a large section of the plate and we therefore need to eat a lot of this type of food.

Activities

▶ After using the photograph, have some of the ingredients available for the children to look at, feel and describe (use the photocopiable page 'Looking and tasting' on page 15 for this activity and add it to the children's process diaries). Firstly, look at the uncooked versions of the carbohydrates then make a comparison with the cooked versions. Rice and pasta (use small shapes) could be cooked in the microwave; couscous should have boiling water poured over it, be covered and left for approximately 15 minutes to cook through.

▶ Discuss the carbohydrates, asking the children what they look, feel and taste like. Model the process of describing the appearance and taste of one of the ingredients. For example: 'This couscous looks like big grains of sand which, when cooked, fluff up to a larger size. It is a yellow colour and is soft and grainy when you put in your mouth.' The children can taste all the samples and record their findings on a chart to add to their process diaries (see below). Help them to observe the differences between the raw and cooked versions of the ingredients.

Name of food	Raw	After cooking
Couscous	looks like big grains of sand	fluffs up to a larger size
Rice		
Pasta		
Potatoes		

▶ Next, the children need to explore the range of ingredients they will add to the rice, pasta or couscous. Have some ingredients available from the following examples: spring onions, red pepper, cucumber, dried apricots, apple, yellow pepper, olives, carrots, celery, tomatoes. Discuss the ingredients: what they are called, where they come from, what they taste like, how their colour and shape can be described and what we need to do before we can add them to the salad. Demonstrate how to prepare the ingredients whilst carrying on with the discussion and asking questions.

▶ Show the children how to prepare the additional ingredients in appropriate ways such as chopping, slicing or grating. (You may want to show the 'Cutting', 'Peeling' and 'Grating' videos at this point as a reminder.) Involve the children in the decision-making by asking questions such as: Would it be better to grate the carrot or chop it into cubes for this salad?

▶ Divide the children into small groups to each prepare a different ingredient. Discuss what preparation is needed beforehand (washing, peeling), which equipment to use (peeler, chopping board, grater, knife, plate, bowl).

▶ When all the ingredients have been prepared, bring them together on one table to discuss the changes and how they look. Put approximately 2 tablespoons (2 x 15ml) of the pasta, rice and couscous in a small dish and add about 1 tablespoon (1 x 15ml) of a different ingredient to each. The children can help with this. The samples will all look different and the children should be encouraged to discuss and evaluate them – what they think each one looks like, what they like and dislike about them – perhaps recording their feelings on the board.

MAKING VEGETABLE SAMOSAS

Photograph: Lunch-box items, Samosa ingredients

Photocopiable page: Making and tasting vegetable samosas   PAGE 19

This activity introduces samosas in the context of other lunchtime snacks. 'Lunch box items' includes a samosa, along with spring rolls, pizza, bruschetta, sandwiches, a wrap, soup, sushi, an apple, orange, sausage roll and raisins.

This simple snack can be used to illustrate different preparation techniques and enable children to experience them by helping to prepare ingredients. There is an opportunity here to look at and taste bought samosas so that all the children will know what they look and taste like. The pastry used around the outside can be filo pastry, spring roll or samosa pastry. The samosa should be baked rather than fried.

Discussing the photographs

▶ Display 'Lunch-box items' and ask the children which items they recognise, and if they ever eat any of these items for lunch. Point out the samosa and challenge the children to predict what a samosa is made from.

▶ Use the photograph of samosa ingredients to discuss the children's predictions. Were they surprised? Point out the pastry (in the photograph this is filo) and ask the children if they know of any other types of pastry. Do they know which herbs or spices are in the photograph (cumin, tumeric and coriander)? Discuss how these affect the taste of the samosa.

Activities

▶ Use the 'Making and tasting vegetable somosas' photocopiable on page 19 to prepare the ingredients and equipment. Explain to the children that they are going to watch how a samosa is made. Before starting, talk through all the different ingredients with the children. The potatoes, onions and carrots could be prepared and cooked beforehand – remind the children what these looked like in the photograph before they were cooked. The children could help with the preparation of the ingredients. Whole spices are exciting to look at, feel and smell before they are crushed to use in the filling.

▶ The folding of the samosa, as outlined on the recipe, can be practised by using a strip of plain paper. The children's paper attempts could be included in their process diaries.

▶ A further activity, once the samosas have been made, is to write down the sequence in which they were made. Children could do this in pairs, with the first child writing down the first step then passing to their partner to write the next step and so on until completed.

▶ There should be a tasting session when the samosas are cooked to record the appearance, smell, flavour and texture of the samosa on the 'Making and tasting vegetable samosas' worksheet. Children could also suggest alternative or additional ingredients such as parsnip.

DESIGN AND MAKE ACTIVITY

DESIGN AND MAKE A SALAD OR SAMOSA

Photocopiable pages: Designing my salad or samosa, Planning my salad or samosa   PAGES 20–21

This activity requires the children to use all the knowledge and understanding from the preceding activities to design and make a salad (or samosa) for their own lunch box.

You may decide that the design and make activity would be best carried out over two or three sessions. The designing and planning done in the first session would enable the chosen ingredients to be available for the second session. The second session would then be for making and the final session for evaluating.

Discussion

▶ Discuss with the children the purpose of the salad or samosa and help them develop their criteria, for example, a vegetarian salad, or a samosa that will fit into their lunch box. Remind the children of all the research they have done and that this should help them with their designing. Remind them that they can include ingredients from each of the four main food groups. Encourage them to select at least one from three of the main groups: bread, other cereals and potatoes; fruit and vegetables; milk and dairy foods; meat, fish and alternatives. They should be taught to use foods from the 'Fats and sugars' group sparingly.

▶ Encourage the children to think back to the different salads they looked at and tasted and how important it was that they looked attractive and people should want to eat them. Discuss the use of different colours of ingredients, different layers and toppings.

Activities

▶ Ask the children to draw and/or describe some ideas they have for a salad or samosa on the 'Designing my salad or samosa' photocopiable on page 20. They may find it helpful to label their ideas, and show them to and discuss them with a partner before reaching a conclusion. The final idea can be drawn and labelled.

▶ Encourage the children to describe what their product will taste like. All this information will form the specification and will help the children evaluate their final product.

▶ When they decided on a product, ask them to complete a plan – this should show the steps and ingredients they will need to produce the salad or samosa. The 'Planning my salad or samosa' photocopiable on page 21 will help them to organise their work.

▶ Allow the children to make their product, following their recipe, method and food safety and hygiene rules. Photograph the outcomes.

EVALUATION

EVALUATING THE SALADS AND SAMOSAS

Photocopiable page: Evaluation   PAGES 22

It is important to allow the children to evaluate their own product and those of their peers.

Discussion

Display all the salads and samosas that the class has made. Do they all meet the design brief – are they all suitable for an item in a lunch box? Discuss the similarities and differences between the products. Identify salads where dressings and toppings have been used effectively to make the salad more flavoursome and appealing. Ask the children to talk about their work to the rest of the class, what they have done and why they did it.

Activities

▶ Ask the children to evaluate their finished product against their original criteria using the 'Evaluation' photocopiable on page 22. They should also consider presentation and taste.

▶ Ask the children to taste each other's work and evaluate it in a similar way. Encourage them to be positive and fair.

Looking and tasting

▶ Draw a picture of your food item in the circle in the middle of the page.

▶ Draw a circle around the words below that show what your food tastes like and how it feels in your mouth.

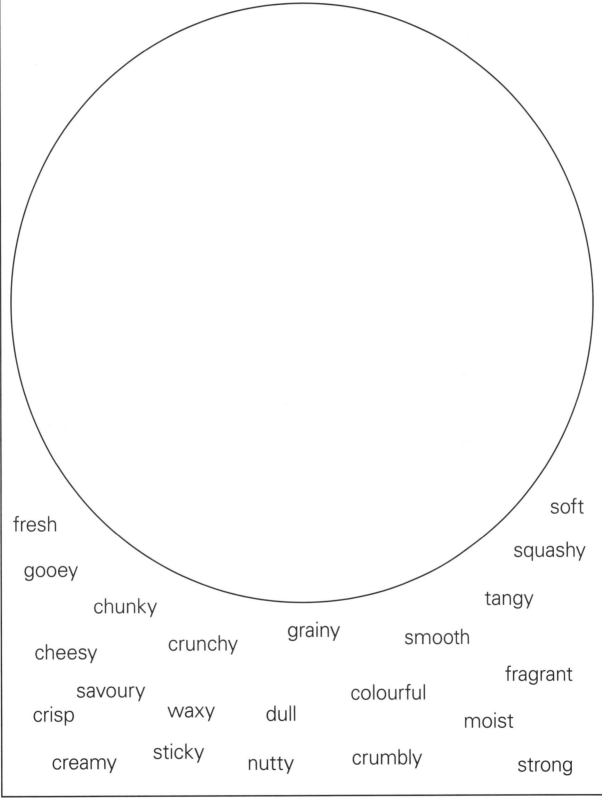

fresh

gooey

soft

squashy

tangy

chunky

grainy   smooth

cheesy   crunchy

savoury   colourful   fragrant

crisp   waxy   dull   moist

creamy   sticky   nutty   crumbly   strong

What's in the salad?

▲ Draw or name the salad in the first column.
▲ List the separate ingredients of this salad in the other columns.
▲ Use the picture of the eatwell plate to help you.

Name of Salad	Fruit and vegetables	Bread, rice, potatoes, pasta	Milk and dairy	Meat, fish eggs and beans	Fats and sugars

◣ SCHOLASTIC
PHOTOCOPIABLE

Evaluating salad ingredients

▲ Complete the table below for each sample of food that you have explored.
▲ Here are some words that you could use: soft, hard, colourful, strong, crunchy, squashy, crisp, stringy, crumbly, creamy.

Name of ingredient	Appearance	Smell	Taste	Texture

SCHOLASTIC
PHOTOCOPIABLE

Create a salad

▲ Invent your own salad.
▲ Draw it in the bowl below and label it.
▲ Remember to use a mixture of different types of food.

Bread, rice, potatoes, pasta

Milk and dairy foods

Fats and sugars

Fruit and vegetables

Meat, fish, eggs, beans

Illustration © Jane Bottomley

■ SCHOLASTIC
PHOTOCOPIABLE

Making and tasting vegetable samosas

Equipment

sharp knife

chopping board

teaspoon

tablespoon

pastry brush

baking tray

saucepan

Ingredients

1 pack filo pastry or samosa pastry
1 onion
1 medium potato
1 carrot
4 tablespoons frozen peas
1 teaspoon (5ml) tumeric
½ teaspoon (2.5ml) ground cumin
½ teaspoon (2.5ml) coriander
4 tablespoons (60ml) vegetable oil

Method

1. Heat the oven to 200°C, gas mark 6.

2. Peel the potato, carrot and onion.

3. Cut or dice the vegetables and put them in a saucepan half-filled with water.

4. Bring them to the boil and simmer them until they are partly cooked.

5. Take them off the heat, drain them and leave them to cool.

6. Crush the spices until fine.

7. Add the peas and crushed spices to the cooled vegetables.

8. Cut or fold a pastry sheet into a rectangle 8–10cm wide, then brush it with a little oil.

9. Place 1 tablespoon of the vegetable mixture at the end of the strip. Fold it over in triangles, sealing the end with oil (see diagram). Repeat until all the mixture is used.

10. Put the samosas on a baking tray.

11. Brush each samosa with oil.

12. Bake for 10–20 minutes until golden brown.

▶ Describe how the samosas:

Look:_____

Smell:_____

Taste:_____

Feel:_____

Illustration © Jane Bottomley

■ SCHOLASTIC
PHOTOCOPIABLE

Designing my salad or samosa

▶ I am going to make _____

Design criteria

1. _____

2. _____

3. _____

▶ Draw and label your design.

▶ What does your friend think about your idea?

_____

_____

_____

▶ Do you need to change anything to make it better?

_____

_____

_____

◼SCHOLASTIC PHOTOCOPIABLE

Planning my salad or samosa

Equipment needed

_____

_____

_____

_____

_____

_____

_____

_____

Ingredients needed

_____

_____

_____

_____

_____

_____

_____

_____

Method

SCHOLASTIC
PHOTOCOPIABLE

Evaluation

▲ You said you wanted your salad or samosa to do these things (copy your design criteria here):

1. _____

2. _____

3. _____

▲ How well does your product do each of these things?
▲ Give your product a mark between 1 and 4 (1 – very good, 4 – not very good). Explain your mark.

_____

_____

_____

▲ What do you think about your final product? _____

▲ What new skills have you learnt? _____

▲ If you were to make this again, would you do anything differently? _____

BAGS

Content and skills

This chapter links to Unit 4A 'Money containers' of the QCA Scheme of Work for design and technology at Key Stage 2. The unit has been amended so that the work is now focused around using textiles to create a bag for a specific user or purpose, taking sustainability into consideration. Children already have experiences of carrying things themselves and seeing other things being carried. They can use this knowledge and experience when evaluating a selection of commercially produced bags; this also helps to generate ideas and set criteria for their own designs.

The chapter is structured as follows:
▶ Investigating: Who uses bags?
▶ Investigating: What makes a bag?
▶ Stitching.
▶ Sketching and modelling.
▶ Generating ideas.
▶ Developing ideas: decorating and finishing.
▶ Design and make activity.
▶ Evaluating their bags.

The children are encouraged to investigate bags, their purpose and who would use them. There are opportunities to discuss issues relating to sustainability in terms of waste, reusing and recycling. The children will also have opportunities to learn techniques to join and reinforce fabrics using a variety of different sewing methods.

Photograph © 2008, Kate Pedlar

Outcome

The main outcome for this unit will be to design and make a bag for a specific user and purpose. In doing this, the children will be expected to:
▶ use information from investigating bags to inform their own designing and making
▶ model their early ideas in paper before committing to a final design
▶ develop their skills in working with textiles
▶ use decorative techniques and finishes to create an individual product
▶ think carefully about how they use materials and keep waste to a minimum, using reclaimed and recycled materials where possible to make their product more sustainable
▶ design and make a bag using appropriate materials and techniques
▶ evaluate critically both the appearance and function of the bag against the original specifications.

Health and safety

When working with sewing equipment, appropriate methods of use should be demonstrated, such as storing pins and needles safely (for example, in a cork to avoid injuries). Children using sewing machines should be supervised. If used bags are being handled, ensure that they are clean.

Links to other subjects

English: discussion about the user and purpose of products, writing and sequencing instructions when planning work, asking questions when evaluating others' work.
Maths: measuring accurately, creating templates by scaling up images.
Art and design: use of textiles, decorative techniques of appliqué.

Organising the unit

All three types of activity should be undertaken (investigating and evaluating, focused practical tasks, designing and making). The order in which they are undertaken can be of the teacher's choosing. For example, starting points could be:
► setting the design and make activity
► looking at a collection of bags – for example, the different bags that children bring to school
► deciding how an assortment of objects from the classroom could be transported home.

Resources on the CD-ROM

The gallery of resources includes photographs of bags used for different purposes by different types of user. These include a handbag, beachbag, child's bag, wicker basket and rucksack. The images will support collections of bags brought in by the teacher or children for evaluation purposes.

There are photographs of fabrics such as leather, felt and knitting to help children understand that different fabrics have different properties. Close-up photographs of specific features of bags show a variety of handles and fasteners to emphasise that function is an important part of the product design. These include hook and loop, buttons and press studs.

Photograph © 2008, Kate Pedlar

Basic sewing stitches for joining seams (running stitch and back stitch) and for simple decoration purposes (chain stitch and fern stitch) have been included as video clips. This will allow pupils to access the images as frequently as they need, thus freeing up the teacher's time to support pupils in other areas.

Photocopiable pages

Photocopiable worksheets in the book and on the CD-ROM include:
► a worksheet for investigating bag designs
► guidance on different types of stitch
► a bag template
► design specification and evaluation sheets for children to set the criteria for their bag design and evaluate their final product against these criteria.

Photocopiable pages on the CD-ROM only include health and safety sheets to support teaching of practical skills such as, 'How to use of scissors'.

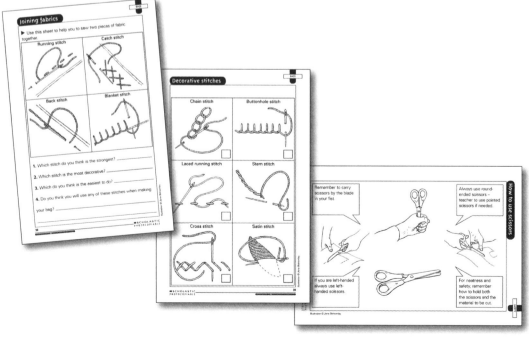

INVESTIGATING AND EVALUATING IDEAS

BAGS: WHO USES THEM?

Photographs: Child's bag, Cool bag, Cyclist's bag, Sports bag, Beach bag, Belt bag, Shoulder bag, Rucksack, Wicker bag, Wicker basket

Photocopiable page: Bag design   PAGE 31

Many children's experience of bags will be carrying a rucksack to school or helping to carry home shopping in plastic carrier bags. The photographs show a wide range of bags used for a variety of different purposes. There are bags which are used as containers to help us carry objects as well as bags that can be carried in different ways by the user – over the shoulder, on a belt or in a hand. The photographs also show that bags are made from different materials and have design features such as pockets and fasteners specific to their purpose.

Discussing the photographs

▶ Look at each picture as part of a slideshow of bags; ask the children what they think each bag would be used for. Discuss situations where they might have seen a similar bag used or may have used one themselves.

▶ Talk about the colour and decoration on each bag and decide if the bag would appeal more to men, women or children. Ask the children to discuss the features of the bag that helped them decide this: was it the colour of the bag, the materials it was made from or were there specific decorative features that were noticeable? For example, compare the child's bag, which is brightly coloured and decorated with pictures, with the cool bag which is very plain. Discuss how the purpose and user of these bags are very different. Have the children also noticed that bags carried by men or boys are usually carried on their backs or over their shoulders, whereas women and girls carry bags in a variety of ways?

▶ Ask the children to look carefully at how the bag has been designed to be carried. Do they think this feature of the bag is an important part of its purpose? Look at the cyclist's bag: how is it different to the other bags? (It fits on the bike, instead of being carried.) Are wide handles essential features of cool bags or sports bags? Encourage the children to think about what the user will be doing at the same time as carrying the bag or what they might be carrying in the bag: the cyclist will need to keep his or her hands free, and frozen food or sports equipment can be particularly heavy, so a bag might need thick straps to help spread the weight.

Activities

▶ Let the children work in groups to brainstorm all the different uses of bags they can think of. Reinforce the terms 'user' and 'purpose' and ask them to consider if a particular type of person would use the bag or if the bag would be used for a particular purpose.

▶ Collect pictures of school bags from catalogues, then ask the children to sort the bags into boys', girls' or either. Look at the colours and styles that make the bags appeal to different genders. Get a few volunteers to bring out the bags they usually carry to school and say why they chose their bag. Discuss the different features of each bag.

▶ Encourage the children to bring in other types of bags to make a class collection. Use this collection to discuss the user and purpose of each bag. Look at how the bag is constructed and any features or decoration on it.

▶ Give the children a bag each to evaluate in more detail. Ask them to fill in their observations on the sheet 'Bag design' photocopiable on page 31, focusing on the user or purpose of the bag, how it is carried and what type of person it would appeal to. This could form part of a process diary.

▶ Ask the children to choose one of the bags from the photographs or from the class collection and write and present a sales pitch for their chosen bag. They should decide who they would want to sell the bag to and why that person would want it. Their sales pitch should include all the important features of the bag. As part of their presentation they could wear the bag and pretend to be that person.

▶ Give the children profiles of different users and ask them to find pictures of bags in

magazines that the user might consider buying. They could make an image board of pictures of bags or specific features that they think that person would want to see in a bag.

WHAT MAKES A BAG?

Photographs: Weaving, Knitting, Shoulder bag, Felt, Buttons, Press stud, Zip, Hook and loop, Drawstring, Buckle, Fabric handle, Ribbon handles

Photocopiable page: Bag design

PAGE 31

To generate ideas for their own designs, children need to look in more depth at the way the bag is made. The materials and textures of the bag, the fastenings and the straps, together with the decoration, are important features as well as functional parts of the bag's design.

Discussing the photographs

▶ Children will usually have had experience of weaving through previous art activities but may have little knowledge of other materials and where they come from. Use the photographs to help explain how weaving is done on a loom with fibres criss-crossing to make a pattern; knitting is made by using needles to pull fibres through each other, which is why if you break one fibre a 'run' appears; leather (see 'Shoulder bag' photograph) is made from animal skins and felt is made when fibres bond together.

▶ Look at the photographs of the fasteners and discuss how each one works: buttons are visible and attached so that they slide through a hole sideways and lie flat; press studs are hidden between layers of fabric, with one part pushing into the other; a zip has teeth that interlink, 'Hook and loop' (Velcro®) has small hooks that attach to fibres and was inspired by nature (by plants that disperse their seeds with hooks and barbs that attach to animal fur); drawstrings pull the fabric together to close it; a buckle needs a strap to go through it.

▶ Remind the children that they have already discussed ways in which bags are carried and show them the photographs of the handles. Discuss how each would feel in their hands. Can the children think of other types of handle? (For example, beaded.)

▶ Talk about ways of attaching fabric to fabric, for example, to attach a handle, or decorate part of the bag – adhesive or stitching are the most likely options.

Activities

▶ Ask the children to think about other items that have fastenings like clothing or shoes. Make a list of the different fastenings that they can think of and where they would be found.

▶ Ask the children to use the photocopiable sheet, 'Bag design' (See page 31), that they previously used to investigate a bag. Explain to them that they are going to add further information by looking at how the bag they chose has been made. Ask them to label their sketch with specific features of the bag, how it is fastened, the decoration on it and how it is carried.

▶ In this activity, the children could choose a different bag or keep the same one as before. If they choose a different bag, they will need another copy of the 'Bag design' worksheet

to fill in. Ask them to look carefully at the structure of the bag. How many pieces is it made from? How are the pieces joined together? Ask the children to find bags with gussets – pieces added to make the bag wider. If the bag is not made of too many parts, they could try to draw the separate pieces.

▶ Let the children have small pieces of each type of material. Give them time to devise ways of testing the fabrics to see which ones would be good to use in their designs. They should consider whether the fabrics will fray when cut, whether or not it will be easy to push a needle through two layers or if any fabrics are too stretchy to keep their shape.

Photograph © 2008, Kate Pedlar

FOCUSED PRACTICAL TASKS

STITCHING

Videos: Running stitch, Back stitch

Photocopiable page: Joining fabrics   PAGE 32

The children will need to practise some cutting and sewing skills to enable them to make a quality product. The video clips will allow them to watch the process of joining fabric much more clearly than a diagram could illustrate. The clips could be set up on a computer or on a whiteboard where the children can access them to watch as many times as they need, giving the teacher the freedom to support other children with their work.

Discussing the videos
▶ Watch each clip in turn to help explain the technique. Point out how it is important to sew stitches of an even length so that the fabric is held together strongly.
▶ Discuss how strong each stitch looks and where it could be used. Running stitch is an easy stitch but not as strong as back stitch, which is a bit more difficult to do neatly.

Activities
▶ Give the children the opportunity to practise their cutting skills by allowing them to use scissors to cut up small pieces of fabric. Make sure they keep these pieces as they can be used for practising different stitches.
▶ After watching the video clips and teacher demonstrations, give out copies of the instruction sheet 'Joining fabrics' from page 32, showing how to join two pieces of fabric together with different stitches. Ask the children to try out each of the stitches on their pieces of fabric. They can then choose which stitches they want to use to join their seams.
▶ Explain how the children can evaluate their stitching skills by asking them to compare their sample to the picture on the instruction sheet and then commenting on their work – how neat it looks, how strong the seam is, how easy or difficult it was to do.

SKETCHING AND MODELLING

Photocopiable page: Template for a bag   PAGE 33

Children will need the opportunity to test out their design ideas through sketching and modelling. Textiles can be an expensive resource to waste so it is a good idea to encourage the children to try out their ideas by modelling with scrap paper first. They can then make as many changes to their designs as they wish.

Activities
▶ Give half the children a copy of the 'Template for a bag' from page 33. Ask them to cut out the pieces and decide which parts they need to join together to make a bag shape. Explain that the gusset is optional but try to make sure that around half the class is making a bag with a gusset. A bag with gusset should be made by more dextrous children. Tell the children to join the edges together with adhesive or staples. The children may have noticed the seam allowance shown as dotted lines on the template. Explain that this is to make sure that the bag is a certain size and that they should keep their adhesive within the space. Children who have made a bag with a gusset should compare their bags with a partner who has made a bag without a gusset to see the differences between the two.
▶ Ask the children to sketch some ideas for other bag shapes. Let them make their own simple templates for their designs from scrap paper which they can cut out and stick together to test. Remind the children that they will need to add a seam allowance to their templates before they cut them out.
▶ Give the children a chance to decorate their different paper bags with their own design.
▶ Demonstrate how to scale up the simple bag template to a larger size. This could be done by tracing the template on small squared paper then copying it on to larger squared paper. It could also be done by measuring the lines and doubling the length of each one as it is redrawn. These templates could be included in the children's process diaries.

GENERATING IDEAS

Photocopiable page: Designing a bag PAGE 34

Children should gather ideas together to help with designing their product; they should consider which materials they could use. With a user and purpose in mind they can then generate ideas for the kind of bag that would meet their criteria. The children should be encouraged to use ideas from their bag investigation activities and to think of several ideas so that they have options to choose from once they have practised some skills needed and considered constraints of time, materials and individual skills.

You could also show children how to make felt (see below). Felt is usually made by overlapping fibres of sheep's wool and bonding them by rubbing them together in hot water and alkali (washing powder). An easy, sustainable alternative is to use old woollen jumpers.

Activities

▶ Collect a range of fabrics from clothing no longer needed but in good enough condition to be reused, for example, denim, cotton, fleece, PVC. Put a collection of different fabrics on each table in the classroom and ask the children to discuss in groups how each could be used. Encourage them to imagine the fabric made into a bag. What kind of user would want a bag made out of this fabric? Are there any parts of the garments that are particularly useful? For example, a jeans pocket could be a pocket on a bag with an added button as a fastener.

▶ Demonstrate how to reuse an old woollen jumper by washing it in hot water to felt the fibres together (see below). Show the children the finished felted fabric and explain what has happened to the fibres. Ask the children to consider what kind of bag the new fabric would make and who might want to use it.

▸ Use wollen jumpers that have a 'handwash only' label in them. Other woollen jumpers that are machine washable have been treated to stop them from shrinking in the wash.

▸ The easiest option is to collect a few woollen items and place them in a washing machine set on a hot wash, 60°C or higher. Add plenty of washing powder and a few tennis balls or old jeans to add more friction to the wash.

▸ If the children are going to felt the jumpers, collect all of the woollen items together and using hand-hot water let the children roll up their sleeves and get rubbing! Large washing-up bowls and rubber gloves could be useful.

▸ When the jumpers have had a good rubbing, rinse them and squeeze out the water.

▸ Pull the jumpers into shape and leave them to dry.

▸ You should now have a fabric that can be cut to shape without fraying.

▶ Discuss with the children the task of making a bag. This could be an open brief with individual children deciding who their bag is for and for what purpose. Alternatively, the brief could be more specific so that all the children are working towards designing a bag for the same user or for the same purpose. In this context the class needs to decide the purpose of the bag or identify someone that they are all familiar with who needs a bag, such as designing a bag to keep the school PE equipment in or to carry a picnic to the park in. Give out the 'Designing a bag' photocopiable on page 34 and ask the children to fill in the essential criteria that they have decided together for their own bag design: for example, the bag must be able to close securely or it must be able to leave your hands free.

▶ Talk to the children about how they can make their bag individual and get them to decide on their own criteria to add to the class list. They might want to consider the shape of the bag, the material it is made from or the decoration on it.

▶ Tell the children to sketch their initial designs. Explain that these are their first thoughts and that they might want to consider several ideas before deciding on a finished design.

Illustration © 2007, Jane Bottomley

DEVELOPING IDEAS: DECORATING AND FINISHING

Videos: Chain stitch, Fern stitch

Photocopiable page: Decorative stitches   PAGE 35

The children will now reflect on the investigations they have done to find out about the shape of bags, fabrics, joining seams and adding fasteners. They need to evaluate some of their initial ideas, considering the constraints of time, materials available and their own skills in stitching neatly before deciding on a final design. They need to try out some of their ideas for decorating and finishing their product to enable them to see what works and what does not and to choose which ideas to take forward to their product designs.

Discussing the video
▶ The videos can be referred to by the children throughout the design and make activity as a reminder of how to decorate fabric using chain stitch and fern stitch.
▶ Point out that the pattern looks neater if the stitches are all the same length and remind the children that decorative stitches are only used on a single piece of fabric, so they need to take care not to sew two pieces of fabric together.

Activities
▶ The children may now have several ideas for bag designs. They need the opportunity to test out decorative techniques to practise their skills and to see if the technique is suitable for their design. Demonstrate appliqué as a method of putting lettering or a bold pattern on their bag design. Show how the pieces can be attached together. An iron-on fabric adhesive can help hold the pieces together whilst it is being more securely stitched. Give out materials for appliqué for the children to try. Ask them to evaluate the technique as a method of decoration.
▶ Show the children how to attach buttons, beads, sequins and so on, either by gluing or stitching them. Give out a few for the children to try to attach themselves, to test out the technique.
▶ Demonstrate a few decorative stitches such as buttonhole or blanket stitch, chain stitch and cross stitch. The children can refer to copies of 'Decorative stitches' on page 35 for guidance. If the children have chosen decorative stitches for their designs, they may like to practise them on small pieces of fabric that they could later mount as a bookmark or card.

DESIGN AND MAKE ACTIVITY

DESIGN AND MAKE A BAG

Photocopiable pages: Bag design, Designing a bag,
Planning sheet   PAGES 31, 34, 36

You may find it useful to set the context of making the bag at the start of the project. This would give the practical skills and design tasks a specific focus. Alternatively, you may prefer to do some investigative activities first so that the children have gathered some information about bags before deciding on the context for designing their own bag. Either way, a clear user or purpose should be presented to the children so that they are making their bag for a real reason. This enables them to make their research more meaningful and gives the final evaluation of their product a clear purpose.

Ideas for the context of the bag may come from the children or from a situation that is familiar to them. Some suggestions are as follows: a bag to carry beach toys on holiday; a drawstring bag to keep a PE kit in; a bag to use when cycling to the park; a bag for the school site manager to put his/her tools in when he/she is working around the school.

Activities
▶ The 'Designing a bag' photocopiable on page 34 can be given to the children at the start of the project, and as they test ideas out they can record them on their sheet. Alternatively, the sheet could be given to the children to complete after all the investigations and practical tasks have been done.

▶ Give out fresh copies of the 'Bag design' sheet and ask the children to review their initial ideas and decide what will work best within the constraints of time, materials and their skill level. Tell them to sketch their final idea on the sheet, showing their choice of material and labelling the specific features mentioned in the design criteria. Ask the children to make a list of all the resources they will need to make their bag so that they can ensure everything is available before they start. These pages can then be added to their process diaries.

▶ Encourage the children to model their ideas in paper by making a mock-up of their design. Explain that this will help them in the next stage which is planning the order in which to proceed with the making. The mock-up can also be used as a pattern for their bag.

▶ Explain to the children the need to plan carefully so that they don't waste resources by making too many mistakes. Give out the 'Planning sheet' on page 36 and encourage them to consider the order in which they will make their bag. Remind them to measure accurately when making their pattern, to add a seam allowance and to transfer their design on to the fabric without creating too much waste. Encourage them to think about the decoration in the planning stage: would it be easier to decorate the pieces once they have been cut out or after they have been sewn together? Remind the children that they will need to refer to and add to their list of resources as they plan their work.

▶ When the children are ready to make their bag, help may be needed. This is a good opportunity to invite relatives in to class to assist with pinning work together or threading needles. The extra help will be invaluable as the children progress at different speeds.

EVALUATION

EVALUATING THE FINISHED BAGS

Photocopiable page: Evaluating the finished bag   PAGE 37

The evaluation process gives the children the opportunity to compare their product against the original design criteria and to assess their skills by identifying areas they are pleased with and highlighting areas for improvement.

Discussion
▶ Display all the finished bags and discuss them as a class. Can the children identify the intended users and purposes for the bags? How many different materials and decorative techniques have been used?

Activities
▶ Ask the children to work in pairs to test out each other's bag. Remind them that they need to evaluate the bag against the criteria set; they need to imagine that they are the user and think how the user would feel if the bag was theirs. Encourage the children to make positive and constructive comments to the maker of the bag. Any negative comments should be backed by a reason, for example, 'I don't think the bag is big enough as my shoes won't fit in it'. 'It is smaller than I wanted because I made the seams too wide.'

▶ Give out the 'Evaluating the finished bag' photocopiable on page 37 and ask the children to fill in comments for each other. They should think about the whole process of designing and making the bag and comment on knowledge and skills that they have acquired during the process.

▶ Give the children the opportunity to present their bag design to the rest of the class. They could stand up and explain who the bag is for and how they have considered their needs when designing it. They could give reasons for their choice of fabric and decoration and ask for comments and opinions from the other children.

▶ Make a display of the children's work showing the whole process from the investigation of bags, deciding on initial ideas, testing out and modifying, through to final designs and making the bag.

Bag design

How is it carried?

How are the seams joined together?

Are there any other special features?

Who is the bag for?

What materials have been chosen?

What fastener is used?

How is it decorated?

SCHOLASTIC
PHOTOCOPIABLE

Joining fabrics

▶ Use this sheet to help you to sew two pieces of fabric together.

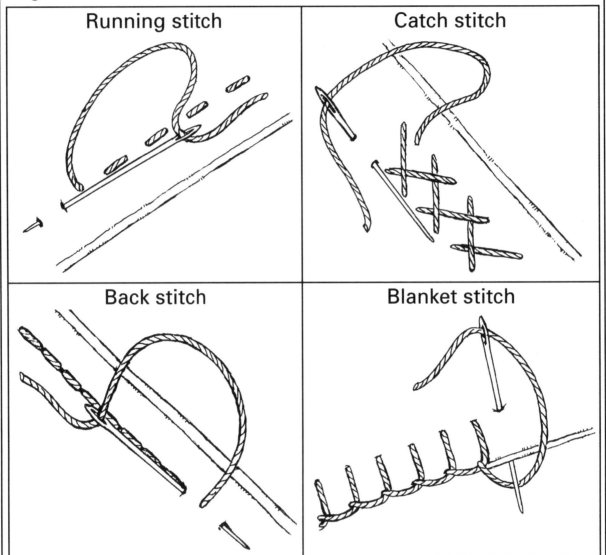

Running stitch

Catch stitch

Back stitch

Blanket stitch

1. Which stitch do you think is the strongest? _____

2. Which stitch is the most decorative? _____

3. Which do you think is the easiest to do? _____

4. Do you think you will use any of these stitches when making

your bag? _____

_____

Illustration © Jane Bottomley

■ SCHOLASTIC
PHOTOCOPIABLE

Template for a bag

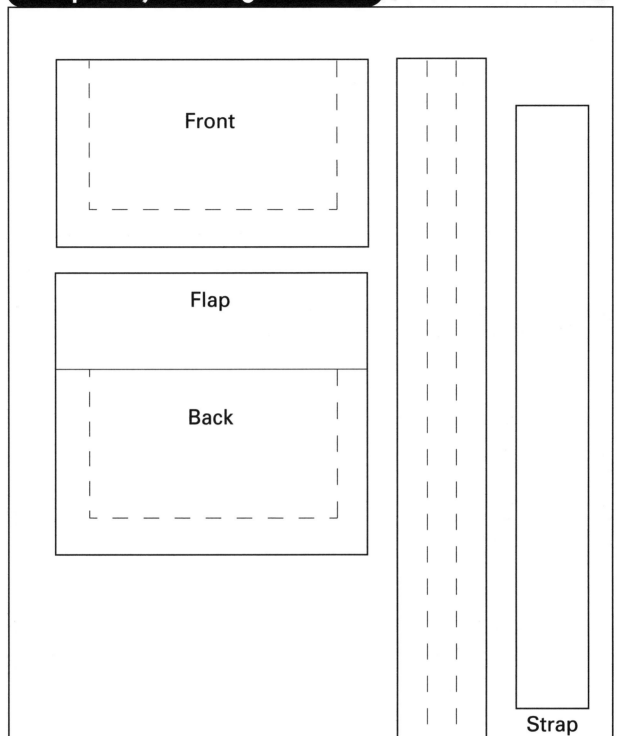

Front

Flap

Back

Gusset

Strap

SCHOLASTIC
PHOTOCOPIABLE

Designing a bag

▶ The bag must:

1. _____

2. _____

3. _____

Who will use your bag?	How will your bag be secured?
What will be carried in it?	Does your bag have different compartments?
What materials will you use?	How will your bag be carried?
What will you use to decorate your bag?	Does your bag have any other special features?

Sketch some ideas for your design here:

◖SCHOLASTIC
PHOTOCOPIABLE

Decorative stitches

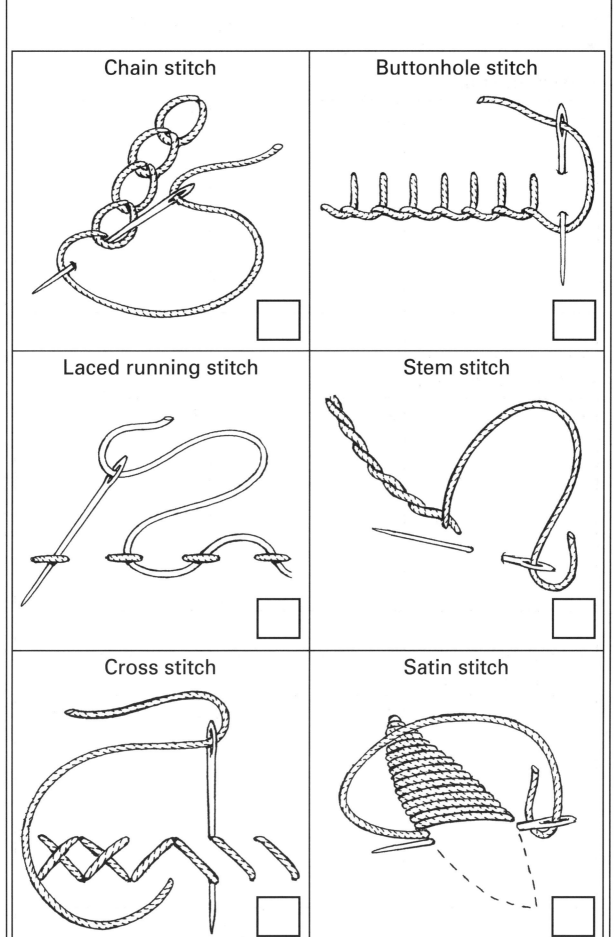

Chain stitch

Buttonhole stitch

Laced running stitch

Stem stitch

Cross stitch

Satin stitch

Illustration © Jane Bottomley

SCHOLASTIC PHOTOCOPIABLE

Planning sheet

▶ Draw pictures to show each stage of making your bag.
▶ Label each picture in the space underneath.

Making the pattern:

1.	2.	3.

Adding the decoration:

1.	2.	3.

Sewing together:

1.	2.	3.

READY RESOURCES ▶▶ DESIGN AND TECHNOLOGY

◼ SCHOLASTIC
PHOTOCOPIABLE

Evaluating the finished bag

Design criteria	Does your bag meet these criteria?
1. _____	1. _____
2. _____	2. _____
3. _____	3. _____

▶ Does the bag hold its contents securely?

_____

▶ Have you used the correct choice of materials?

_____

▶ Is the style and decoration suitable for the user?

_____

▶ What new skills or knowledge have you learnt?

_____

▶ How do you feel about your product?

_____

▶ Ask other people for their opinions.

Name: Opinion:
Name: Opinion:

SCHOLASTIC
PHOTOCOPIABLE

READY RESOURCES ▶▶ DESIGN AND TECHNOLOGY

PHOTOGRAPH FRAMES

Content and skills

This chapter links to Unit 3D 'Photograph frames' of the QCA Scheme of Work for design and technology at Key Stage 2. The main focus of this chapter is materials and their properties, although children will also learn that materials can be manipulated and combined to make them stronger. They will be introduced to techniques to create strong frame structures and learn that wide bases can give structures their stability. Children will have opportunities to create decorative features for a frame by combining materials which are then used to enhance a picture being displayed. They will also learn that the choice of materials or techniques will depend on the user or purpose of the product.

There will be opportunities for children to generate their own ideas for designing a frame by investigating commercial products; they will look at the use of displays in the wider environment and test out ideas of their own through sketching and modelling. Children are encouraged to demonstrate a sustainable attitude by using materials responsibly. To avoid creating too much waste, reused card and paper is suggested.

The chapter is structured as follows:
▶ Investigating stability.
▶ Investigating photograph frames.
▶ Investigating the need for frames.
▶ Cutting and manipulating paper and card.
▶ Combining materials.
▶ Design and make activity.
▶ Evaluating their photograph frames.

Photograph © 2008, Kate Pedlar

Outcome

The main outcome for this unit will be to design and make a picture frame for a specific user and purpose. In doing this, the children will:
▶ gain an understanding of the ways in which structures can be made stable
▶ research materials that could be used to construct photograph frames
▶ identify who the user might be and what the user needs and wants in the frame
▶ generate some possible solutions to the user's needs/ wants
▶ design and make a complete personalised photograph frame, appropriate for a particular person.

Health and safety

In this chapter, the children learn skills in cutting and scoring accurately with appropriate tools. Ensure that the children carry scissors closed with blades in their palms and that they score away from their bodies. Refer to your school and local authority health and safety policies and guidance for the safe use of sharp equipment. When investigating frames, ensure that they are in good repair and have no sharp edges. Children must take care with any frames that have glass in them.

Links to other subjects

English: discussion about the user and purpose of products, writing and sequencing instructions when planning how to make a frame and asking questions when evaluating others' work.

Maths: measuring accurately and ensuring rectangular frames are made with right-angle corners.

Art and design: decorative techniques including collage and mosaic.

Organising the unit

All elements of the unit should be covered but the order in which they are covered can be of the teacher's choosing. For example, starting points could be:
▶ investigating how to make something stand up
▶ investigating how to display special things
▶ investigating a collection of picture frames
▶ listening to the audio files.

Photograph © 2008, Kate Pedlar

Resources on the CD-ROM

Photographs on the CD-ROM show collections of picture frames used in the home. Photographs of frames with a variety of different finishes and decorative techniques will help the children to generate ideas for their own designs. Photographs of different decorative techniques are shown in some of the pictures. To help the children consider different users of photograph frames, a collection of audio files have been included: the children can listen to people talking about their favourite picture, why they would like to frame it and what sort of frame they would be looking to buy.

Photocopiable pages

Photocopiable pages in the book and on the CD-ROM include:
▶ investigating structures and frames worksheets
▶ planning and designing sheets to help children organise their thoughts and ideas
▶ an information sheet providing starting points for children to learn about strengthening materials.

Photocopiable pages on the CD-ROM only include and health and safety sheets and a set of word cards.

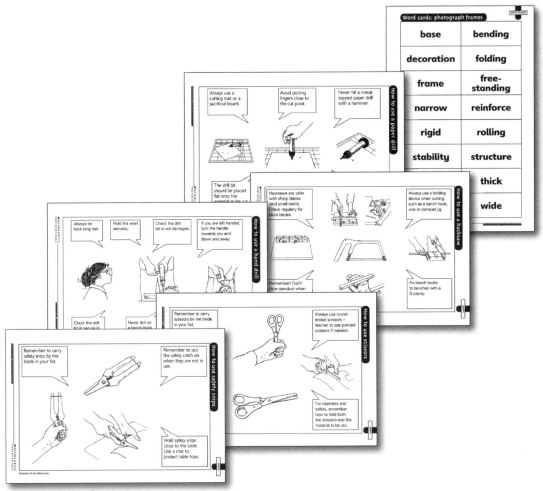

INVESTIGATING AND EVALUATING IDEAS

INVESTIGATING STABILITY

Photographs: Music stand, Deck chair, Sun lounger, Privacy screen, Cube, Pyramid

Photocopiable page: Investigating stability   PAGE 46

By looking at photographs of familiar structures, children learn why stability can be an important consideration in the design. Key examples of structures to include in discussion are those with wide or heavy bases, or those which have triangular bases for stability. Most of the photographs from the gallery of resources show frame structures, but also included are two images of 3D shapes to show that shell structures are stable too. This will help the children to be more creative when designing their own photograph frames. They will learn that there are other ways of making a frame stand up besides using a simple A-frame design.

Discussing the photographs: materials
▶ Make a slideshow of the music stand, deck chair, sun lounger and privacy screen. Looking at each photograph in turn, discuss with the children where they might find each of the objects. Ask the children if they can recognise the materials the object is made from and explain to them that they are all structures made from frames.
▶ Some materials in the frames are solid like the wood on the deck chair; others are hollow tubes as in the music stand. Look at the item made from tubular metal and ask questions to focus attention on how the material has been altered or processed to make it more useful. Can the children explain why the music stand is made of tubular material (so it is lighter to carry and durable)?

Discussing the photographs: structures
▶ Discuss with the children what each structure is designed to hold and how each structure holds it.
▶ Some of the items in the photographs, such as the deck chair and music stand, have been designed to fold away. Ask the children to point out the parts of the structures that might be hinged to allow them to fold. Talk about why these structures need to be folded away (they are structures which are not needed all the time; because of their wide base they take up a lot of room in storage). Folding items flat makes it easier to pack them into boxes to be sold in shops.
▶ Look at the photographs of the cube and pyramid shapes which have been included in this collection of stable objects and discuss why they have been included. Ask the children to think about what makes a 3D shape stable (its wide base). They should consider the shape of the base of the 3D structure and whether it would make any difference to the stability of the shape if it was standing up on a different shaped side. Ask the children to think of other 3D shapes that could have been included in the collection.

Activities
▶ Ask the children to work in groups and brainstorm structures. What things can they see around them that are made to stand up? Ask them to think about whether the structure holds something up or in place. They should consider how the structure is made stable, what kind of base it has and what materials it is made from.
▶ Give the children the 'Investigating stability' photocopiable on page 46 showing pictures of other stable objects that they may be familiar with. Ask them to label the part of the object that is stable and explain in the space provided on the sheet why the object needs to be stable and what could happen if the structure was not stable.
▶ Using components from a construction kit, ask the children to work in pairs to make a stable structure. The task could be open, giving the children an opportunity to make any kind of structure they choose, or it could be more specific such as asking the children to make a piece of playground equipment or a book stand. Ask the children to sort their structures into those with a wide base and those with triangular bases.
▶ Ask the children to test stability by timing how long they can stand on one foot without

wobbling, then compare this with how much better they can stand on two feet spread out.
▶ Provide photocopies of the 'Word cards: photograph frames' (CD-ROM only) (base, bending, decoration, folding, frame, free-standing, narrow, reinforce, rigid, rolling, stability, structure, sturdy, thick, thin, wide). Ask the children to explain where the words would be used.

INVESTIGATING PHOTOGRAPH FRAMES

Photographs: Photograph frames, Beaded mirror, Metal frame, Plastic frame, Stone frame, Back of frame, Cube

Photocopiable page: Investigating frames   PAGE 47

Photograph frames come in all different shapes and sizes and are made from a range of materials. A photograph frame needs to incorporate a way of putting the picture behind the frame so that it can be removed and changed if needed. The choice of frame could depend on the picture that is going into it or where the frame is going to be displayed. The choice of frame might also depend on the preferences of the user and the style they like, whether they prefer traditional designs or more contemporary ones.

Discussing the photographs
▶ View each of the photographs of the frames as a slideshow: the collection shows a selection of frames of a variety of shapes, sizes and materials, all designed to hold photographs. The images can act as a supplement to a collection of frames brought in by the teacher or children. As each photograph is viewed, ask the children to consider the user of the frame. Who would want to buy it and where they would keep it?
▶ Look closely at each photograph and discuss what materials the frames could be made from. Look at the photographs of the frames, especially their shape. Ask the children why they might be different shapes. One of the frames has a pressed leaf inside: challenge them to work out if this would have fitted in any of the other frames.
▶ Ask the children to try to imagine what kind of picture each frame could display. Would a picture of a person look better in an oval frame or a rectangular frame? Which one of the frames do they think would suit a picture of a landscape?
▶ Look at the photograph of the back of a frame. Discuss whether the frame is designed to stand up on a shelf or hang on a wall or could it do both? (This frame has a stand and a hook, so could do both.) Explain how some frames have a space to slide the picture in and other frames have a piece at the back which comes off to fit the picture in, show how this then needs to be held in place with clips (as in the 'Back of frame' photograph). Look at where the support is joined on by hinging and discuss how this has been designed to fold flat.
▶ Look at the decoration on each frame. Discuss how it might have been done. Ask the children which frames they prefer and why.
▶ Show the 'Metal frame' photograph which has cats and fish bones on it. Ask the children who they think would buy this frame and what kind of picture they think would look good in it.
▶ Discuss the 'Cube' photograph and explain that some photograph frames are shaped like this. Does anyone have one at home? Although it does not have a frame around the picture, the frame is the cube itself as it is the shape that supports the images. Ask the children to think of other 3D shapes that could be used to display photographs in the same way.

Activities
▶ Ask the children to bring in photograph frames from home to create a class collection. Put a selection of the frames on each table and ask the children to work in groups to investigate the frames. They should investigate how each frame stands up: can they work out what makes it stable? Ask them to look at how the picture is inserted into the frame. Encourage them to look closely at the decoration and decide whether the frame has been made of decorated material or whether the decoration has been added to the frame later. Take care with photograph frames that have glass in them.
▶ Give out photocopies of the sheet 'Investigating frames' on page 47 and ask the children to choose one of the frames to sketch. Tell the children that they will need to draw the frames from the front, side and back to show the structure of the frame and how it stands up. Ask them to label the important parts of the frame, the material it is made from, any decoration,

where the picture goes in and how it stands up.

▶ Ask the children to list items that could be used to make a collage. Set up some containers in the classroom and ask the children to start collecting items and bring them in from home, for example, shells, magazine pictures, beads, pasta.

▶ Give the children pages from magazines or catalogues and ask them to cut out pictures to make a class image board of photograph frames. Explain how they can group pictures together to show frames made of similar materials or frames that would fit into similar settings. Put the board on display in the classroom as a reference point for the children to use to generate ideas for their own designs.

INVESTIGATING THE NEED FOR FRAMES

Photographs: Beaded mirror, Certificate, Window, Door, Noticeboard

Photocopiable page: Blank frame template   PAGE 48

Before designing their frame, the children need to understand why frames are used. Frames are used in many ways: to make something stand out and to guide the eye to something worth seeing; to protect something important and to stop the edges being worn away; for decoration, to add more interest to an object. Point out that frames are usually a rigid structure.

Discussing the photographs

▶ Look at the photograph of the mirror. Discuss why mirrors often have frames around them. Ask the children to think about what they see when they look in the mirror and where mirrors are usually placed. Discuss the fact that the mirror is made from glass and that glass might need protecting with a frame. Discuss how a mirror can be fixed to a wall; glass can be screwed if it is specially drilled but often a frame is used to help keep the mirror in place on a wall.

▶ Using the photographs of the window and door with frames around them, discuss what might happen if a window or door had no frame. How would the glass be kept in place? How could the door hinges be fixed to allow the door to open and close freely? Ask the children to think about the materials windows and doors are made from. Can they explain why these materials are used and how they think they are joined to make right-angled corners?

▶ Show the photograph of a framed certificate to demonstrate that frames are used to make something special stand out. Framing something also allows it to be pinned to a wall or stood up on a shelf so that it can be displayed for people to see. Discuss with the children what might happen to a painting or certificate over time if the frame was not there.

▶ Look at all the photographs and explain to the children how the frames are all rigid structures. They are usually made of solid wood or metal or tubing.

Activities

▶ Give the children copies of the 'Blank frame template' on page 48 and ask them to cut the frame out carefully, particularly the middle of the frame. Ask the children to hold the blank frame up and look around the room or out of a window to create a scene in the frame. Let the children describe their scene to a partner.

▶ Ask the children to put their frame near a friend's face to see how it would look if their friend's picture was in a frame. Get them to move the frame away from themselves for a head and shoulders view, or ask their subject to move further away for a full length view. Ask a few children to pose together so that other children can frame them in the picture.

▶ Collect a few leaves or petals from the school grounds. Give them to the children to arrange inside their frame to make a nature picture. Let the children walk around the class looking at the pictures that others have made.

▶ Tell the children to work with a partner and ask each other questions about their interests and hobbies. They should also find out what colours and patterns their partner likes. Using crayons, the children can then decorate their blank frames with colours, patterns or pictures that they know their partner would like. When they have finished decorating their frames, they can ask their partner for their opinion.

FOCUSED PRACTICAL TASKS

CUTTING AND MANIPULATING PAPER AND CARD

Photocopiable pages: Strengthening card, How to use a hacksaw (CD-ROM only), Words cards: photograph frames (CD-ROM only)

PAGE 49

Children will need to practise skills in measuring, scoring and cutting so that they can make their frame neatly and with the strength needed for it to be a stable structure. They should be given the opportunity to find ways to make flexible materials, like card, more rigid. This can be done by folding and rolling card into beams and tubes. Discuss the safe use of tools – how to handle scissors safely and using saws correctly if wood is to be used.

Discussion

▶ Remind the children of the photographs of structures that they looked at earlier. Explain how the frames were all rigid structures made of solid wood or metal or tubing. Explain how sheet materials can be folded or rolled to make square or round tubing, and tell the children that they will be able to try out some of these methods with card.

▶ Remind the children how to use scissors safely: they should always carry scissors closed, with the blade in their fist (see 'How to use scissors' on the CD-ROM). When scoring, they should ensure that the card is firmly secured with one hand.

▶ If wood is available, the children will need to use a hacksaw to cut the wood to size. Refer to 'How to use a hacksaw' on the CD-ROM and your school's health and safety policy for guidance.

Activities

▶ Show the children how to measure and mark out strips of card neatly, then let them practise by making their own to use in the following activities. Provide pieces of scrap card from cereal boxes or similar lightweight packaging and ask them to use a ruler to draw some lines 5cm apart and some 10cm apart. Ask them to cut the strips out neatly for a class 'store'.

▶ Give out the photocopiable 'Strengthening card' on page 49 and allow the children to follow the instructions on the sheet to score and fold strips of card to create more rigid structures. Ask the children to devise a test to find out which methods of folding create the strongest strips.

▶ Give the children a selection of tapes and adhesives to join card. Let them work in pairs to find ways of joining their card strips together neatly. Ask them to find ways of joining two strips of card to make a right-angled corner and show them how to use a corner piece of card as a right-angle tester. (Push the card inside the corner and check that there are no gaps between the card and the corner created.)

▶ If square-sectioned wood is available, the children should be given the opportunity to practise marking out, sawing and joining small pieces of wood using a jointing frame.

▶ Give the children images of people cut out from magazines, ask them to stick the pictures on to scrap card. Give out some strips of scrap card, a selection of adhesives and sticky tape and equipment that could be used to help make the card stand up such as string, pipe-cleaners, lollipop sticks, paper clips and plasticine®. Ask them to find different ways of making the card people stand up. Remind the children of their previous work looking at stable structures and making card more rigid by folding and rolling.

▶ Give the children paper to record sketches of their models or use a digital camera to record their work. The pictures can then be used as part of a class display using words from the 'Word cards: photograph frames' on the CD-ROM to label their models or images.

COMBINING MATERIALS FOR DECORATION

Photographs: Mosaic, Nut collage, Magazine collage

Photocopiable page: Frame designs

PAGE 50

The children will have the opportunity to model their ideas and record them with sketches showing different views and perspectives. Using their knowledge of materials, they will then test out their ideas for making a frame in card (mock-ups). They will explore materials that

they could use as decoration, and model covering their frames using different decorative techniques.

Discussing the photographs

▶ Show photograph of the mosaic and draw the children's attention to the fact that the pieces are a uniform size with only small gaps between them. Stress the fact that the mosaic doesn't have to be a picture, mosaic patterns can look just as effective.

▶ Look at the photographs of the nut collage and the collage made of magazine cuttings. Discuss how the pieces have been placed close together or overlapped to cover an area. Explain to the children how the decoration looks more effective by keeping to the same theme and not mixing different images or objects together.

▶ Can the children think of any other materials for collage? Discuss printing, where the same image is produced over and over again. Ask the children about their experiences of printing. Discuss papier mâché and the use of mouldable materials to cover the frame. Discuss how the material is made, how it is used and how it could be coloured when dry.

Activities

▶ Give the children an opportunity to try out some of the decorative ideas discussed. Provide them with collections of materials suitable for collage work, such as magazines, shells, pasta shapes or rice, and allow them to try out the materials by covering a small piece of scrap paper or card. They could use a photocopy of the blank frame (see page 48) and try out a different decorative technique on each corner.

▶ Give out copies of the 'Frame designs' photocopiable on page 50. Ask the children to consider the different aspects of their frame and fill in the four sections of the sheet. Explain that this is an opportunity to consider lots of different ideas. They can then evaluate each other's ideas, leading to a decision on their preferred design.

DESIGN AND MAKE ACTIVITY

DESIGN AND MAKE A PHOTOGRAPH FRAME

Photocopiable page: Final design   PAGE 51

Audio files: Children, Football, Travelling, VE Day

This activity gives the children the opportunity to design and make a picture frame for a specific user and purpose. The children can use their knowledge of joining and reinforcing card to make it suitable for the job it has to do. The following tasks are designed to take the children through activities which support elements of the design and technology process that develop key knowledge, skills and understanding to enable them to successfully design and make a picture frame.

Before the children begin to generate ideas for their own designs, they need to have a reason for making a photograph frame. It may be useful to give the children a design brief so that while they are practising some of the practical tasks needed to make a frame, they are already considering who will use it, what sort of photograph will go in it and where the frame will go. The brief can be very specific; the children can be asked to design and make a free-standing frame for a particular person or place suggested by the teacher, or the brief can be more open-ended so that the children are asked to design ways of displaying a special picture for a particular person of their own choosing.

Audio files from the CD-ROM are available so that the children can listen to different users talking about their need for a photograph frame. The teacher could use one or all of these characters to set the brief. The characters have been chosen to link in many ways to the children's own experiences; they may have studied life during the Second World War as part of their history work, or they may have grandparents with memories of the war. Most families have holiday photographs at home as well as collections of baby pictures and many children are keen sports participants.

Discussing the audio clips
▶ Listen to the different people talking about their special picture. Ask the children to work in pairs and jot down notes about the person. How much information do they know about this person in the short audio clip they have heard?
▶ Take each person individually and ask the children to discuss what features they want in a photograph frame. Ask the children what clues they picked up from the audio clips: the mother, for example, wants a frame for her daughter's bedroom, which she describes in detail; the traveller wants a frame that reflects the places he has visited.

Activities
▶ Choose children to role play the characters from the audio clips, using prepared notes as a prompt. While they are in the 'hot seat' other children could ask them questions to help them decide on design ideas for a photograph frame. Referring back to the slideshow of photograph frames, the children could choose a frame to suit each character, suggesting any adaptations they might make.
▶ Ask the children to invent some characters of their own to add to the role play, imagining a picture that person might have and where they would want to put a photograph frame.
▶ You may want to discuss the design criteria at this point and allow the children the opportunity to complete the first part of the 'Final design' sheet on page 51. The remaining parts of the sheet can be completed when the children have had more experience of practical tasks and been given the chance to practise some techniques and model some of their ideas. This should become part of their process diaries.
▶ Review the criteria for designing a photograph frame; they may need reminding of who the frame is for, what features it must have, what kind of picture will be displayed in it and where the frame will go. Will it need to stand up or will it be displayed on the wall?
▶ Ask the children to think carefully about their final design and complete the 'Final design' sheet on page 51. They will need to consider all the ideas they have tested out and generated from the investigation activities. Discuss any constraints the children will need to work with, such as, the materials available; the time allowed to make the frame; decorative techniques. Encourage them to use the ideas that they know worked well and discard ideas that they found were not so good. Make sure that the children annotate their design sheet to show the materials they want to use and explain the important features of the frame design.
▶ Remind the children about the safe use of tools: see the sheets on the CD-ROM and refer to your school's health and safety policy. Ask them to collect together the materials they need to make the structure of their photograph frame. Remind the children to keep referring to their design sheet and to remember the design criteria as they make their frames.

EVALUATION

EVALUATING THE FINISHED FRAMES

Photocopiable page: Evaluating the finished frame   PAGE 52

The evaluation activity is an opportunity for the children to present their solution to the task by showing others their work.

Discussion
▶ Find out what the children think they have learned throughout the project. What skills have they developed? What have they learned about materials and structures?

Activities
▶ Ask the children to present their work to the class: they need to explain the criteria for their frame, how well they think they worked, which aspects of their work they were particularly proud of and which, if any, they found difficult. Invite the children to comment constructively on each other's work.
▶ Give out the 'Evaluating the finished frame' photocopiable on page 52 and ask the children to fill in their comments and those of others.

Investigating stability

► Label the part which makes each structure stable.
► Explain why it is important that each object is stable.

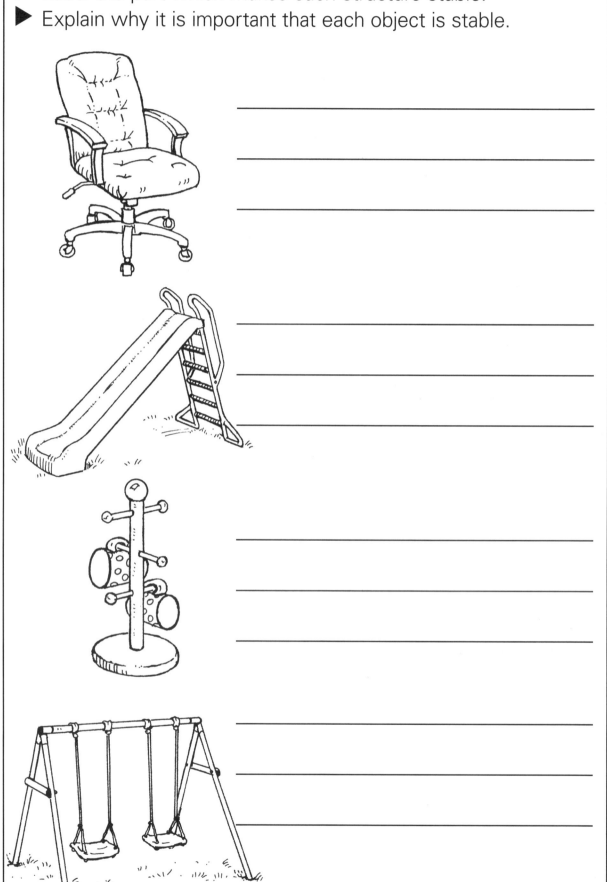

_____

_____

_____

_____

_____

_____

_____

_____

_____

_____

_____

Illustration © Jane Bottomley

■SCHOLASTIC
PHOTOCOPIABLE

Investigating frames

▶ Choose a photograph frame to sketch.

Front view:

1. What materials have been used?

_____

2. Who would want to use this frame?

_____

3. What decoration is on it?

_____

Back view:

4. How is the picture put in?

_____

5. How have the parts of the frame been joined?

_____

6. What decoration is on it?

_____

Side view:

7. How does the frame stand up?

_____

_____

8. Is the structure stable?

_____

SCHOLASTIC
PHOTOCOPIABLE

Blank frame template

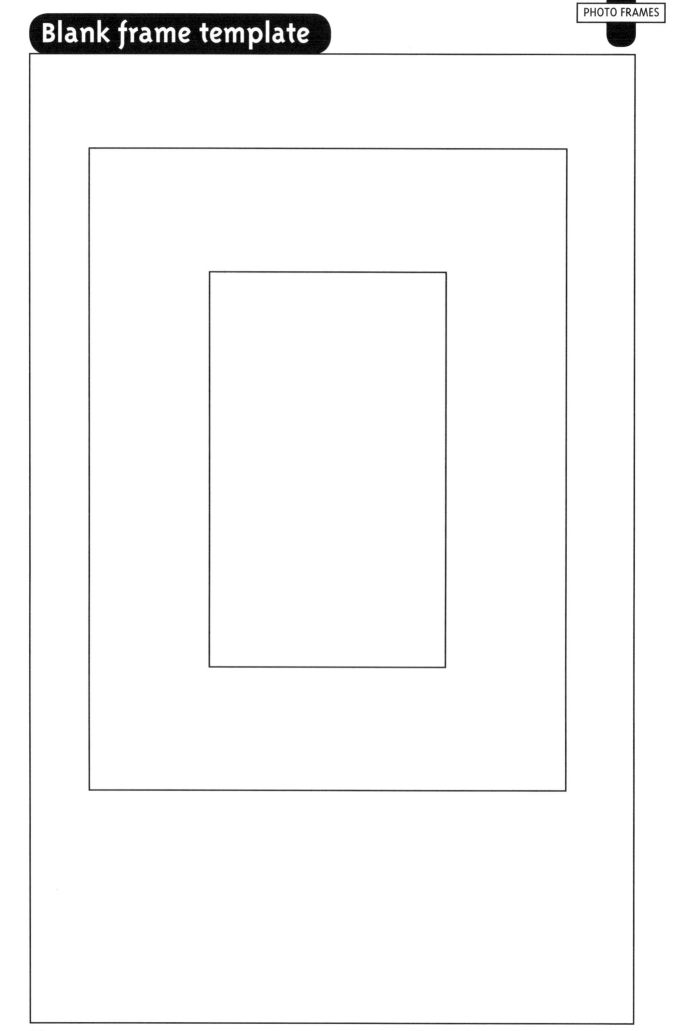

■ SCHOLASTIC
PHOTOCOPIABLE

Strengthening card

▶ Cut some strips of scrap card 5cm x 15cm or 10cm x 20cm.

▶ Try different ways to make the card stronger and more rigid by folding or rolling it.

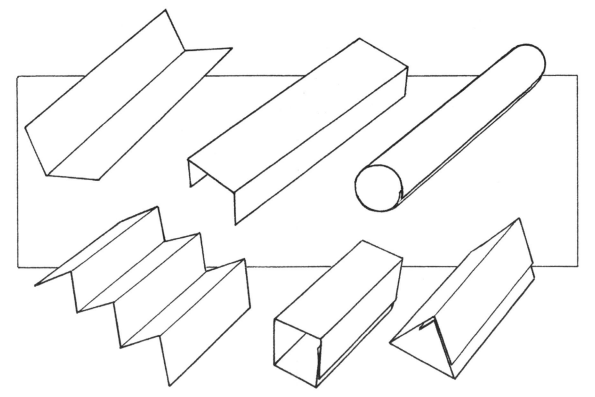

▶ Now test some of your structures to find out which is the strongest.

▶ Draw the strongest structure in the space below.

Illustration © Jane Bottomley

◢ SCHOLASTIC
PHOTOCOPIABLE

Frame designs

▶ Sketch an idea for your frame in the boxes below and add labels.

▶ You will need to think about:

  ▶ the shape of your frame;
  ▶ how you will make the frame;
  ▶ how your frame will stand up;
  ▶ how you will decorate your frame.

Shape	How it is made
Structure	**Decoration**

▶ Which do you think is your best design? Explain why.

_____

_____

_____

◣ SCHOLASTIC
PHOTOCOPIABLE

Final design

► Design criteria:

1. _____

2. _____

3. _____

4. _____

► Who is your frame for?

_____

► What picture will go in it?

_____

► Where will the frame be put?

_____

► Sketch your frame design here and label any important features.

► Materials needed:

► How will you make the frame?

_____

► How will you join the parts of the frame together?

_____

► How will it stand up?

_____

◢ SCHOLASTIC
PHOTOCOPIABLE

Evaluating the finished frame

Design criteria	Does the photograph frame meet your criteria?
1. _____	1. _____
2. _____	2. _____
3. _____	3. _____
4. _____	4. _____

▶ What are you pleased with? Is there anything you would

change?_____

_____

▶ Have you used the correct choice of materials?

_____

_____

▶ Is the style and decoration suitable for the user?

_____

_____

▶ What new skills or knowledge have you learnt?

_____

_____

▶ How do you feel about your product?

_____

_____

◀ SCHOLASTIC
PHOTOCOPIABLE

STORYBOOKS

About the unit

This chapter links to Unit 4B 'Storybooks' of the QCA Scheme of Work for design and technology at Key Stage 2 and the main focus is control: mechanisms. The activities encourage children to look closely at the content and layout of the moving illustrations in books. These illustrations should include those that use lever or linkage mechanisms. The children will have opportunities to look at and discuss existing products with moving mechanisms.

The chapter is structured as follows:
▶ Investigating mechanisms.
▶ Exploring mechanisms: pop-ups.
▶ Exploring mechanisms: sliders, levers and linkages.
▶ Design and make activity.
▶ Evaluating their storybooks.

Outcome

The main outcome of this unit will be to design and make a storybook from card, with a particular user in mind, which shows part of the children's picture moving using a lever or linkage mechanism. In doing this, the children will be expected to:

Illustration © 2007, Jane Bottomley

▶ investigate and evaluate products with lever and linkage systems and learn how they function
▶ explore how different mechanisms can be used to produce different types of movement
▶ cut and shape materials and components with some precision to allow a mechanism to function
▶ model a design proposal in a variety of ways
▶ identify the audience and purpose of a book
▶ use tools safely and effectively
▶ design and make a storybook with a particular purpose and user in mind.

Health and safety

When working with tools, it is important to demonstrate safe and appropriate usage, such as carrying scissors with blades held in the fist, facing downwards and keeping fingers away from the sharp parts of brass fasteners. Refer to your school's health and safety policy for guidance, before allowing children to use tools.

Links to other subjects

English: The activities require skills such as questioning, describing and speaking and listening. The children will have opportunities to read words related to work on mechanisms, tools and equipment and they should be encouraged to use the correct terminology at all times. The children will also have opportunities to: practise different styles of handwriting when presenting their final storybooks; work together to write a creative story with a particular audience in mind; take notes; plan; brainstorm ideas and think about different ways of presenting their work; be creative and to think about possible solutions to problems.
Science: The children need to understand the concepts of friction and balanced and unbalanced forces in order to create effective sliders and levers.
Art and design: There are opportunities to practise drawing and to explore the effects of different visual elements: colour, shape, texture and so on.
ICT: The text or illustrations for the storybooks could be created using a computer.

Organising the unit

All elements of the unit should be covered, but the order in which they are covered can be of the teacher's choosing. For example, starting points could be:
▶ exploring how to present a class reader in a different way
▶ investigating a collection of storybooks
▶ setting the design and make activity.

Resources on the CD-ROM

The gallery of resources contains photographs and videos clips demonstrating different products that use mechanisms to create movement: a see-saw, a wheelbarrow, a door handle, windscreen wipers and a lever bridge. These examples can be used in conjunction with products and examples of pop-up books collected by the class.

Also on the CD-ROM is a selection of illustrations. These can be discussed as a class and ideas gathered as to how the illustrations can be made more appealing by adding a pop-up element. The illustrations include well-known characters, such as Little Red Riding Hood, or fit into the popular topic themes of 'The Seaside' and 'Vehicles'.

Photocopiable pages

Photocopiable pages in the book and on the CD-ROM include:
▶ Investigating mechanisms and pop-up books.
▶ Generating ideas: pop-ups.
▶ Generating ideas: levers and linkages.
▶ Design a storybook.
▶ Storyboard.
▶ Evaluation.

There are also support sheets on the CD-ROM only:
'Word cards: storybooks', 'How to use scissors'
and 'How to use a paper drill'.

INVESTIGATING AND EVALUATING IDEAS

INVESTIGATING MECHANISMS

Photograph: Windscreen wipers
Videos: Door handle, Wheelbarrow, Tower Bridge

Photocopiable pages: Investigating mechanisms, Investigating pop-up books, Word cards: storybooks   PAGES 59, 60

It is important that the children are able to explore and evaluate existing products that demonstrate different types of movement. They need to understand that mechanisms create different types of movement. Video clips and images on the CD-ROM show mechanisms in action and will help develop children's understanding of them. The children need to consider the users and purposes of each type of example. They should be encouraged to identify the type of movement in each product and to explain how they think it works. The children could then be given opportunities to look around the classroom and school to see if they can identify objects that use mechanisms to create movement.

Discussing the photograph
Show the photograph of the windscreen wipers. Ask the children to explain what the photograph shows. Can the children explain how the windscreen wipers move? Introduce the terms 'lever' and 'pivot'. Can the children think of anything in the classroom or at home that works by using a lever and a pivot? For example, scissors or a wheelbarrow.

Discussing the videos
▶ Start by showing the video clip of the door handle. Ask the children if they can tell what mechanism has been used and what movement it creates. Challenge the children to identify the moving part and explain how it works. (The handle is the lever and as this is pushed downwards, the bolt is pulled inwards.) Explain that this is a fixed pivot: the door handle does not move away from the door.
▶ Show the video clip of the wheelbarrow and ask the children how this is different to the door handle. (It has a bigger lever and pivot and has a load in the middle; the wheelbarrow is able to move.) Explain that this is an example of a loose pivot. Ask the children to identify the mechanism in the wheelbarrow and door handle (levers and pivots).
▶ Look at the video of the Tower Bridge as an example of levers on a larger scale. Can the children think of any other examples of big levers being used elsewhere? (Diggers or level crossings, for example.)
▶ Ask the children to explain the different users and purposes of the levers they have seen. Discuss how this has affected the scale and design. (For example, the lever bridge is functional, but it is also intended to look impressive and grand for visitors. A lot of money would have been spent on the bridge's design and appearance. It is made out of very strong material because it needs to last a long time. In contrast, the wheelbarrow is used in a garden and so doesn't need to look as impressive as the bridge. It needs to be strong enough to hold heavy garden materials, but not as strong as a bridge.)

Activities
▶ Use the 'Word cards: storybooks' on the CD-ROM to familiarise the children with the main words associated with mechanisms and designing and making a moving picture (criteria, fixed pivot, joint, lever, linear, linkage, loose pivot, model, rotary, slider).
▶ Using the 'Investigating mechanisms' sheet on page 59, ask the children to draw one product they have discussed and label the different parts. This could form part of a process diary.
▶ Create a class collection of pop-up books and cards. Ask the children to identify what each moving part does, how it works and the effect it has. The children should consider how well it works, whether it helps in the telling of the story, how the parts are joined together. Do the children like moving books? If so, why? Encourage them to think about how they could use these types of moving parts in their own design ideas. Ask the children who they think would read the book or card. How can they tell?
▶ Give out copies of fiction and non-fiction books with moving parts and ask the children to

evaluate them, drawing the moving parts and showing how they move with the help of the 'Investigating pop-up books' worksheet on page 60. When evaluating, prompt the children with questions such as: Who is it aimed at? What sort of age? What mechanism has been used? Is it effective? How are the parts joined together?

▶ Give the children a non-moving book and ask them to compare it to a moving book. Which parts could they make move? Do they think this would improve the book for the reader? How could they make the moving part?

▶ Draw the class back together and have a class discussion about what the children have found out. Draw up criteria for a successful moving storybook. What do the children think is important? What should the book contain? How should it be organised? Should all the pictures move? Should there be different mechanisms to make things move in different ways? What is the purpose of the book? Who is it for? The children could choose the three most important criteria and add these to their 'Design a storybook' sheets on page 63. Alternatively, a list of the criteria could be kept and re-visited at a later date when the children start to design and plan their own storybooks.

FOCUSED PRACTICAL TASKS

EXPLORING MECHANISMS: POP-UPS

Photocopiable pages: How to use scissors (CD-ROM only), Generating ideas: pop-ups 　　　　　　　　　　　**PAGE 61**

Through the following tasks the children learn how to make their own pop-up pages. This will involve cutting, scoring and sticking card. When scoring card, fold it so that the score line is on the outside. Ensure the children put a mat or a piece of thick card on the table to prevent it from being scratched. Refer to 'How to use scissors' (CD-ROM only) for safe usage.

Keep all models and prototypes as these will form part of the children's recording of activities in their process diaries. Children may also find it beneficial to refer back to these during the final stages of making. Some children may require templates to support them or ready-made pictures for them to cut out. Some children can print images off the computer. Have glue sticks available to use.

Discussion

Demonstrate how to make a simple pop-up page by folding a large illustration and attaching it across a folded page. (Refer to 'Generating ideas: pop-ups' on page 61 for ideas.) Refer back to the class collection of pop-up books and cards and identify where this mechanism has been used. Discuss how this mechanism can be used to aid a story, for example, a scary monster leaping out of the page at the reader.

EXPLORING MECHANISMS: SLIDERS, LEVERS AND LINKAGES

Photograph: Levers and linkages 　　　　　　　　　　　　　　

Photocopiable pages: Generating ideas: levers and linkages, How to use a paper drill (CD-ROM only), How to use scissors (CD-ROM only) 　　　　　　　　　　　**PAGE 62**

Through the following tasks the children learn how to make their own sliders and linkage mechanisms using card and construction kits. This will involve cutting, and using a hole-punch or hand drill and brass fasteners to create the levers and linkages. Sheets on the CD-ROM provide guidance on how to make these mechanisms and how to use equipment safely.

Again, keep all models and prototypes as these will form part of the children's recording of activities in their process diaries and it may be useful to refer back to them during the final stages of making. Store resources centrally and allow children to start modelling their ideas using card. Ensure card strips are readily available for those children that need them. Some children may require templates to support them or cut-out photocopied pictures. Some children can print images off the computer. Have plenty of brass fasteners available to use.

Discussion

Show the photograph 'Levers and linkages'. Demonstrate how to make a simple slider and lever mechanism with a fixed pivot. (Refer to 'Generating ideas: levers and linkages' on page 62 for ideas.) When you have done this, ask the children to consider how they could use this mechanism to make something move, what they could put on the end and how it could be fixed. Refer back to the class collection of pop-up books and cards and identify where this mechanism has been used. Using an existing product, ask the children to predict what will happen if a lever is pulled: what will happen if I slide this? How can I make this jump?

Activities

▶ Allow the children to make their own simple pop-ups using card.

▶ Give them plenty of time for cutting, scoring and sticking. Refer to 'How to use scissors' for guidance on safe usage.

▶ Allow the children to make up their own situations, such as a bear leaping out of the page, or a ball being thrown. They should sketch their ideas on the photocopiable 'Generating ideas: pop-ups' on page 61 to add to their process diaries.

▶ Ask children to share their work and evaluate it as a class: discuss how the examples work, how effective they are and what can be done to make them more effective. Take photographs and add them to the children's process diaries.

▶ Allow the children to make their own simple lever mechanisms using construction kits or card and fasteners. Can they make fixed and loose pivots? Some children may be able to explore different types of mechanisms.

▶ Have some card strips readily available for some children to use and allow them to place pictures on their lever, so any problems of joining can be discussed. Children could print out a clip art picture and stick it on to the moving part.

▶ Give the children plenty of time to practise using the hole-punch or paper drill over a piece of wood or cutting mat. (Refer to the CD-ROM for guidance on safe usage of tools.) Ensure that the children have plenty of practice at punching holes accurately.

▶ Allow the children to make up their own situations, such as a mouse popping out of a hole, and to trial them. They should sketch their ideas on the 'Levers and linkages' worksheet on page 62 to add to their process diaries.

▶ When using fasteners to create a moving part, ask the children if they notice anything. What happens if the fasteners are too tight or too loose? How can it be improved?

▶ Ask the children to share their work with the class, talking about who the product was made for and how it works. Evaluate these together, discussing how the examples work, how effective they are and what can be done to improve them. Again, take photographs and add them to the children's process diaries.

DESIGN AND MAKE ACTIVITY

Photocopiable pages: Design a storybook, Storyboard, Planning you work **PAGES 63–64**

When designing and making their storybooks, the children must be given a design brief: it is important that they know the purpose and user of their moving storybook. You may decide that the whole class should work on different sections of the same story to produce a class book, rather than individual books.

Children should be evaluating throughout the whole design process. Reference to their final design and planning sheet should be made when the children are constructing their models. Their final product should look like their design. Any changes or modifications should be noted on their design sheets. Make sure that the children realise that they can change their ideas as they develop. The children can refer to the worksheets in their process diaries for guidance on levers and linkages.

Design briefs could include designing and making the following: a storybook for Year 2 pupils: this could be a retelling of a well-known story, or a story of their own; storybook based on a history topic they are studying, for example, The Tudors; a moving picture with a special message for a particular audience, for example, sustainability, environmental issues or healthy eating.

Discussion

Before starting the design and make activity, remind the children of the tasks they have already completed and of the different ways that pop-ups, levers and linkages can be used. Remind the children of the tools, equipment and materials that they may use, and ensure that they know how to use these safely. It is advisable to store resources centrally and label them clearly. Give the children their design brief and explain that they need to consider the user of their product carefully when they consider their design. They should also include the details of the book such as; author, title and page numbers. Revisit or display the key vocabulary they have learned and encourage them to use the correct terminology at all times.

Activities

▶ Ask the children to complete the 'Design a storybook' sheet on page 63. They should set relevant criteria, depending on who the book is for, and list what they will need and draw the different mechanisms they will use on the pop-up pages. Encourage them to think about tools, techniques, joining methods and dimensions. They may also want to interview the user to find out what their needs are: this can then form part of their design criteria.

▶ The children will then need to plan their work carefully using the photocopiable 'Storyboard' on page 64. This should include any text to go on each page and whether the picture is going to be static, a pop-up, or include a lever/linkage mechanism. The children need to consider how they are going to cover any levers and linkages and whether this will mean that the backs of some of the pages will need static pictures or pop-ups, rather than another linkage.

▶ When the children have planned their books, they should make a prototype in paper to ensure that their plan works. This can then be given to a partner, or shared in a group, and amended as necessary.

▶ Ask them to plan the order in which they will carry out their work with the help of the 'Planning your work' photocopiable on page 65. They can use words and/or pictures in their plan. This should be added to their process diaries.

▶ Give the children time to make the final product, reminding them to think about good quality finishing techniques, such as carefully chosen colours, bold images, accurate cutting, neat gluing, no pencil lines showing.

▶ Take photographs of the final products for the process diaries. These can also be used for display or in the evaluation.

EVALUATION

Photocopiable page: Evaluation   PAGE 66

It is important to allow the children to test their products and those of their peers. They should celebrate their work and what they have learned, as well as consider what they would do differently if they were to make a similar product.

Discussion

▶ Look at the final books and determine whether or not the children have fulfilled the design brief. Ask them if it is obvious who the books are intended for. They should consider if a range of different pop-ups, and lever and linkage techniques have been used and whether or not they aid the telling of the story.

▶ Discuss any problems that the children encountered and how they resolved them. Did many children have to modify their designs after they made their prototypes?

Activities

▶ Allow children time to test their product with its intended client and get feedback on it. Were their products successful? Did their products meet the brief?

▶ Ask the children to complete the photocopiable 'Evaluation' on page 66, including a comment from a tester, or the intended user.

Investigating mechanisms

▶ Draw one product you have seen or discussed as a class.
▶ Label the pivot, lever, linkage and mechanism.

Investigating pop-up books

▲ Draw a page from a fiction pop-up book and a non-fiction pop-up book.
▲ For each page, label the mechanism and describe how the different parts are joined together.

Fiction book

1. Who is the book aimed at? _____

2. What age are they? _____

3. How does the pop-up help to support what is written on the page? _____

Non-fiction book

1. Who is the book aimed at? _____

2. What age are they? _____

3. How does the pop-up help to support what is written on the page? _____

◣ SCHOLASTIC
PHOTOCOPIABLE

Generating ideas: pop-ups

▶ Here are two ideas for pop-up pictures.
▶ Draw two ideas of your own in the boxes below.

Idea 1

Idea 2

SCHOLASTIC
PHOTOCOPIABLE

Illustration © Jane Bottomley

Generating ideas: levers and linkages

▶ Here are some ideas for pictures using levers and linkages.
▶ Draw two ideas of your own in the boxes below.

 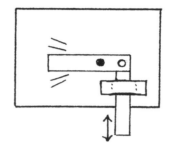 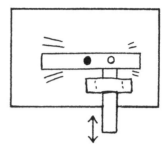

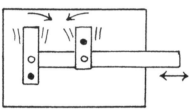 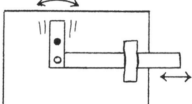 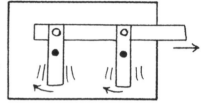

● fixed pivot
○ loose pivot

Idea 1

Idea 2

Illustration © Jane Bottomley

■ SCHOLASTIC
PHOTOCOPIABLE

Design a storybook

Design criteria

1. _____

2. _____

3. _____

▶ Will the pictures be hand-drawn or created on a computer?

_____

▶ Will your book be handwritten or typed?

_____

▶ Draw the different mechanisms you will use inside your book (pop-ups, levers, linkages, sliders). You should include at least one example of levers and linkages.

Storyboard

▲ Plan your book using the storyboard below.

▲ Remember, you will need to cover the back of the page where you have used levers and linkages.

Therefore, you will not be able to use levers and linkages on every page.

▲ Your illustrations and pop-ups should support what is happening in the story.

SCHOLASTIC
PHOTOCOPIABLE

Planning your work

▶ Write the order in which you will do the work in the flow chart below.

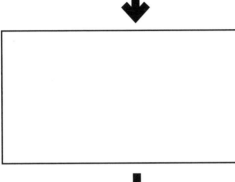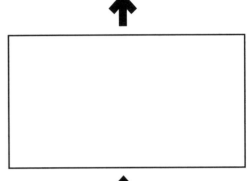
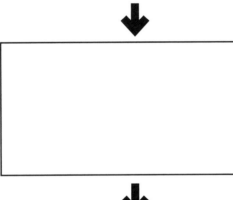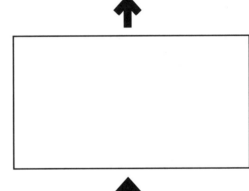
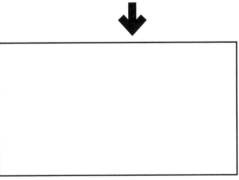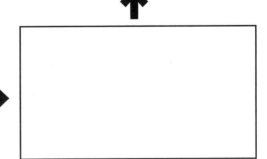

▶ What equipment will you need? _____

_____

_____

Evaluation

How well does your final design meet the criteria that you set?

1.

2.

3.

Criteria

1.

2.

3.

▲ What do you think of your storybook?

▲ What did your tester/user think of your design?

▲ How could you improve your design?

◗ SCHOLASTIC
PHOTOCOPIABLE

LIGHTING IT UP

Content and skills

This chapter links to Unit 4E 'Lighting it up' and 4C 'Torches' of the QCA Scheme of Work for design and technology at Key Stage 2. In this chapter, children will learn about electrical circuits and control technology and the users and purposes of a product that lights up. Children are encouraged to think about the range of users of products that light up and the particular needs that lights have been designed to meet, for example, a night light for a baby's room, a table decoration for a celebration or lighting around a poster in a shop window to advertise an event. This chapter encourages children to think about lights in general: when a light might be used, whether or not all lights hang up, and the fact that some are hand-held, while others need a stand.

The chapter is structured as follows:
▶ Investigating products that light up.
▶ Communicating ideas.
▶ Understanding circuit diagrams.
▶ Using control software.
▶ Design and make activity.
▶ Evaluation.

Outcome

The main outcome of this unit will be to design and make a product which lights up for a specific user and purpose. In doing this, the children will be expected to:
▶ investigate a range of products that light up
▶ research a range of products that light up by collecting torches, lamps, night lights and a range of pictures
▶ consider a wide variety of user needs
▶ design a product that lights up with a specific user in mind
▶ design, make and evaluate a product that lights up
▶ become familiar with constructing an electric circuit in a 3D prototype
▶ explore a range of switches suitable for use with their product
▶ write a sequence of instructions to control their alarm with a stand-alone control box.

Photograph © 2008, Kate Pedlar

Health and safety

The children will need to use a range of practical skills: they will need to cut wire for their products and they may also be involved in cutting card, using a junior hacksaw and bench hook or using a hand drill. Refer to your school's health and safety policy before allowing children to use tools.

Remind the children of the dangers of working with electricity before embarking on any work involving circuits and batteries.

Links to other subjects

Science: this unit links to the QCA Scheme of Work for Science (Unit 4F 'Circuits and conductors'). Children should learn that:
▶ a complete circuit is needed for a light to work
▶ a circuit needs a power source and that batteries are to be used for investigation and experiment
▶ some materials allow electricity to pass through them
▶ some materials are better conductors of electricity than others
▶ a switch can be used to make or break a circuit to turn things on or off
▶ care needs to be taken when components in a circuit are changed to ensure bulbs/motors do not burn out.

English: skills such as questioning, describing, speaking and listening are required. The children will have opportunities to read words related to electrical circuits and products that light up and will be invited to write about how they construct their products as well as record their results from tests.

Organising the unit

All elements of the unit should be covered but the order in which they are covered can be of the teacher's choosing. Starting points could be:

▶ investigating and evaluating different types of products that light up

▶ exploring teacher-made examples

▶ extending science investigations on electrical circuits.

Resources on the CD-ROM

The gallery of resources includes photographs of different types of lights. These images are intended to supplement a collection of actual lights made by the teacher and class. The images can be used for discussion purposes if some types of products that light up cannot be collected and investigated first-hand. The lights can be looked at with different users in mind and evaluated accordingly.

Photocopiable pages

There are a range of photocopiable pages in the book to support the process of creating products that light up. These can be completed by the children to form a process diary or enlarged for wall displays.

Photocopiable pages on the CD-ROM only include 'Word cards: lighting it up', and support sheets for teaching children practical skills, such as the safe use of hand drills, hacksaws, wire strippers and safety snips.

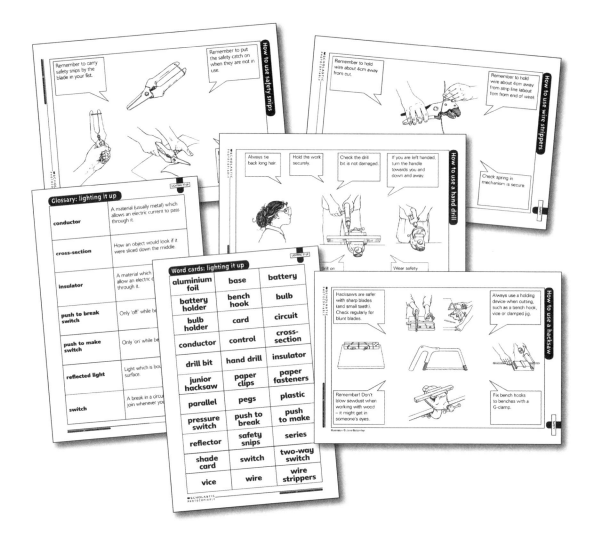

INVESTIGATING AND EVALUATING IDEAS

INVESTIGATING AND EVALUATING EXISTING LIGHTS

Photographs: Torch 1, Torch 2, Torch 3, Cycle lamp 1, Cycle lamp 2, Cycle lamp 3, Cyclists at night, Table lamps, Miner's lamp, Camping lamp, Christmas tree lights 1, Christmas tree lights 2, Christmas tree lights 3, Blackpool illuminations

Photocopiable pages: Investigating lights 1, Investigating lights 2 PAGES 73–74

It is important that the children are able to explore and evaluate existing products that light up. This could be a class collection of lights, teacher-made examples and photographs from magazines. Use the photos on the CD-ROM to support and extend the range of lights to be investigated. The children could do further research via the internet, reference books and CD-ROMs and by collecting pictures from home. Make sure throughout the discussions that the user, purpose and how the light fulfils the purpose are considered.

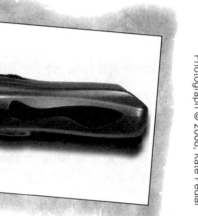

Photograph © 2008, Kate Pedlar

Discussing the photographs

▶ Discuss and compare the different types of torches. Ask the children to explain how they can tell they are all torches. (For example, they are all hand-held, they are made of strong materials, they don't need to be plugged in, they can be carried easily.) Discuss how they are different, even though their purpose is similar. Discuss the advantages and disadvantages of the small torch on a key ring, comparing it to the others. (It can be carried around very easily but may not be as bright.) You may want to discuss the camping lamp at this point as another example of a light that is carried from place to place – although this also has a handle for hanging the lamp outside a tent.

▶ Display the 'Cyclist at night' image. The purpose of a cycle lamp is similar to that of a torch, but ask the children how it needs to be different. (It can't be carried by hand – the cyclist needs to have both hands on the handle bars.) Look at the other cycle lamp photographs and discuss how they are attached to a bicycle.

▶ Look at the table lamps and discuss how they are different to the torches. Can the children explain why they are used as table lamps? (They are more decorative, they need to be plugged in, they have a base to stand on.) You could also discuss the miner's lamp at this point as another example of a light that needs to be transported but leaves the hands free.

▶ Display the Christmas tree lights. Ask the children how these differ from the other lights. Do they think they are more functional or decorative? Ask the children which examples of Christmas tree lights they prefer and what their Christmas tree lights are like at home. Discuss how baubles and tinsel are also often hung on Christmas trees to reflect the lights and make the tree seem even brighter. You could go on to discuss Christmas or other lights in the streets. Display and discuss the 'Blackpool illuminations' photograph at this point.

▶ Lead a general discussion on the lights: Which are decorative rather than functional? Which are expensive and which are cheaper to make? How does the purpose of the light affect the choice of materials?

Activities

▶ Create a class collection of lights – including teacher-made examples if possible. Take photographs of these or print out images from the CD-ROM and create a wall display listing their properties. For example, a torch is hand held, made of plastic, contains a switch, gives out a bright light, can be used when camping or walking.

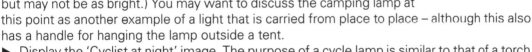

▶ Look at individual lights in more detail and identify: where the switches are, what they are made of, how they are used, where they are used and their suitability for the purpose.
▶ Encourage the children to investigate the lights to answer these questions: how is the light reflected? How does the switch work? Are batteries used and, if so, how many? What type are they? What materials have been used and why? How does the base provide stability?
▶ Organise the children into groups of three to five and ask them to complete the 'Investigating lights 1' photocopiable on page 73. The activity requires the children to choose a light and write down the five most important points in a specification that the designer might have worked to. They then need to sketch and label an observational drawing of the light to include: materials, decoration, moving parts, switches and handles or attachments if appropriate. Extend the activity by asking the children to complete the 'Investigating lights 2' photocopiable on page 74. The children are required to draw one type of light and label it. They are then asked a series of questions which will draw on their investigative skills.

FOCUSED PRACTICAL TASKS

MAKING A CIRCUIT

Photographs: Disassembled torch, Circuit components, Circuit diagram, Series diagram

Photocopiable page: Faulty circuits   PAGE 75

A key aspect of this unit is for children to be able to construct a circuit including a switch. Some children may experience difficulty in designing their own circuits and switches and will therefore need support. The photographs on the CD-ROM show the components needed to make a circuit and the diagrams indicate how these components should be fitted together. At this stage, use either manufactured switches or simple switches that you have created yourself.

Discussing the photographs
▶ Display the 'Disassembled torch' photograph. Ask the children if they can name any of the parts of the torch. Draw their attention to the bulbs, wires and switch. (This example is a wind-up torch and includes a motor at the front of the circuit board. The bulbs are at the back of the green circuit board. The switch is white and is in the centre of the circuit board.)
▶ Discuss with the children the components of a simple circuit, using the 'Circuit components' photograph – wires, 1.5v bulb, 1.5v battery and switch.
▶ Display the 'Circuit diagram' and 'Series diagram' photographs to show the children how to make a circuit. These can be left on the board for reference or printed from the CD-ROM.

Activities
▶ Make a circuit and show the children how it works.
▶ Discuss with them some of the problems that may occur that prevent their circuit from working, such as wires not being connected properly.
▶ Read through the 'Faulty circuits' photocopiable on page 75 and ask the children to fill in the blank boxes. (Answers: Replace the bulb; Tighten screws and check wiring or replace holder.)
▶ Ask the children to create a circuit of their own using wires, a bulb and a battery. The children should now include a manufactured or teacher-made switch in their circuit. Allow some time for them to experiment with a variety of switches in their circuits.
▶ Take photographs of the completed circuits, or ask the children to draw circuit diagrams, to add to their process diaries.

SWITCHES

Photographs: Micro-switch, Push switch, Reed switch, Slide switch, Switches, Toggle switch

Photocopiable pages: Switches, How to use scissors, How to use wire strippers, How to use safety snips **PAGES 76**

Before starting practical tasks, ensure that the children know how to use equipment safely. Sheets on the CD-ROM provide guidance on how to use scissors, wire strippers and safety snips. These can printed out and given to the children to refer to as necessary.

Discussing the photographs

▶ In the previous activity the children made circuits and tried out different switches. Look at the photographs and ask the children which switches they have used and if they can explain how they work.

▶ A micro-switch is activated by the physical motion of a mechanical device such as a lever. When pressure is applied to the lever or button the switch completes the circuit. When pressure is removed the metal strip springs back to its original state. Common applications of micro-switches are computer mouse buttons and joysticks and buttons in arcade games.

▶ A reed switch is operated by an applied magnetic field. Common applications are sensors for doors where the magnet holds the reed away from the circuit so circuit is not complete.

▶ A push switch is an electrical switch that completes the circuit when pressed. When the pressure is removed the circuit is then broken. Common applications of push switches are door bells, key pads on calculators, money dispensers.

▶ A toggle switch is an electrical switch that you move in one direction to complete the circuit and the other to break the circuit. Common applications are light switches, switches on electrical heaters.

▶ A slide switch slides into a position to complete the circuit. It can be used to complete more than one circuit (one at a time) or used with a motor to change its direction of movement. MP3 players use slide switches to allow you to scroll through the music files.

Activities

Ask the children to make a variety of switches by using simple classroom materials (card, plastic, aluminium foil, paper fasteners, paper clips) They should refer to the 'Switches' sheet on page 76. Demonstrate how to make switches that work in different ways, for example, by pressing or sliding. The children should note which switch they prefer and which they find the easiest to make before incorporating a switch into their circuit.

USING CONTROL SOFTWARE

Photograph: Christmas tree lights 1

Inclusion of this section will depend on the availability of resources such as control boxes and a suitable program. Computer control covers Design and Technology and ICT requirements. Control technology can be used if the children decide to design and make a light product that can be turned on and off in a sequence, for example, Christmas tree lights.

Discussion

Discuss why you might want to use a program that allows lights to be turned off and on automatically or in sequence. Show the photograph and discuss that, although in the picture the lights look static, they could be programmed to do other things (twinkle, turn on and off at different times, alternate between white lights and red lights). Ask the children to think of other lights that might be programmed (disco lights, lights on fairground rides and so on).

Activities

▶ Demonstrate how to make a device turn on and off using a control box/program. Remember to change the 1.5v bulb in their circuits to a larger voltage (6v) when using a control box.

▶ Challenge the children to use their own circuits to turn the light on and off in a sequence using your chosen ICT tool.

DESIGN AND MAKE ACTIVITY

DESIGN AND MAKE A LIGHT

Photocopiable pages: Word cards: lighting it up, Glossary: Lighting it up (CD-ROM only), Design sheet, Planning sheet, How to use scissors (CD-ROM only), How to use wire strippers (CD-ROM only), How to use safety snips (CD-ROM only), How to use a hand drill (CD-ROM only)   **PAGES 77–78**

This activity allows the children to design and make a light of their choosing or, alternatively, you may choose to focus on a specific kind. Ensure that the children consider the purpose and user when designing their light.

The investigating and evaluating activities and focused practical tasks enable the children to acquire the knowledge and skills to complete the design and make activity. These can be taught before undertaking the design and make activity or during it where necessary. Before starting practical tasks, ensure that the children know how to use equipment safely. Sheets on the CD-ROM provide guidance on how to safely use scissors, wire strippers, safety snips, hand drills and junior hacksaws. These can printed out and given to the children to refer to.

Design briefs could include designing and making the following: a light to be used during a celebration, for example, a light for Divali, a table decoration for Christmas; a night light for a child's bedroom; a light for a particular user and purpose.

Activities
▶ Explain to the children that they are going to design and make a light for a particular purpose or person. They will need to use what they have learned in the focused practical tasks and investigating and evaluating activities to design and make their lights.
▶ Encourage the children to identify what they want their lights to do, who will use them and where they will be used. Emphasise that their lights will run from a battery not the mains supply. They should add these details to a copy of the 'Design sheet' on page 77.
▶ They will need to consider the user, purpose, design criteria, size, the position of the circuit and switches and joining methods they will use.
▶ Encourage the children to plan what they will need to make their design idea, and outline the different stages of making using the 'Planning sheet' on page 79.
▶ They need to think about the tools and materials they will use and the order in which they will make the different elements. Reference to their final design and planning sheet should be made when the children are constructing the light. Some children will need support when constructing the circuits and switches.
▶ Use a digital camera or movie maker to film their work. These recordings could be used to help other groups and to support other teachers.

EVALUATION

Photocopiable page: Evaluation   **PAGE 79**

Discussion
Display the different types of lights that have been made, then test them. Find out if each light works. In their evaluations, the children should consider if their light can be used in the situation it was designed for. Questions to consider include: Does it stand up safely or hang securely? Can it be carried comfortably? Is it neatly decorated and finished to a high quality?

Activities
The children should use the 'Evaluation' photocopiable on page 79 to record their evaluations against the original design criteria. They should then add the completed sheets to their process diaries.

Investigating lights (1)

▶ What do you think are the five most important features of a light? List them below:

1. _____

2. _____

3. _____

4. _____

5. _____

▶ Now draw one of the lights you have discussed and label the five important features.

▶ How has this light been made safe to use?

_____

_____

■SCHOLASTIC
PHOTOCOPIABLE

Investigating lights (2)

1. How is the light reflected?

2. How many batteries are used?

3. What type are they?

4. Does the base provide stability? If so, how?

5. Can you adjust the light in any way?

▲ Draw one type of light in the space below.
▲ Label the different parts including: materials, decoration, moving parts, switch, bulb, reflector and any handle or attachments.

SCHOLASTIC
PHOTOCOPIABLE

Faulty circuits

► Check all the components you are using by building a circuit to light a bulb. If the bulb does not light, follow these steps to find the fault.

► Two remedies are missing. Can you work out how to sort out the problems? Write your answers in the gaps in the table.

Cause of fault	Remedy
Poor electrical contact	► Turn the batteries in their holders or wiggle them about. ► Move the crocodile clips and press them firmly in position. ► Screw the bulb firmly into its holder. ► Tighten any loose screws on the crocodile clips and the bulb holders.
Faulty bulb	
Dead battery	Replace the battery
Batteries incorrectly connected	If two batteries are used, turn one round so that the negative is connected to the positive.
Faulty clip	Tighten the screws on each crocodile clip or replace the clip.
Faulty bulb holder	► ►

► If you have tried all of these steps and your circuit still does not work, you could have two pieces of faulty equipment. Test each of your components in a completely new circuit that you know is working.

■ SCHOLASTIC
PHOTOCOPIABLE

Switches

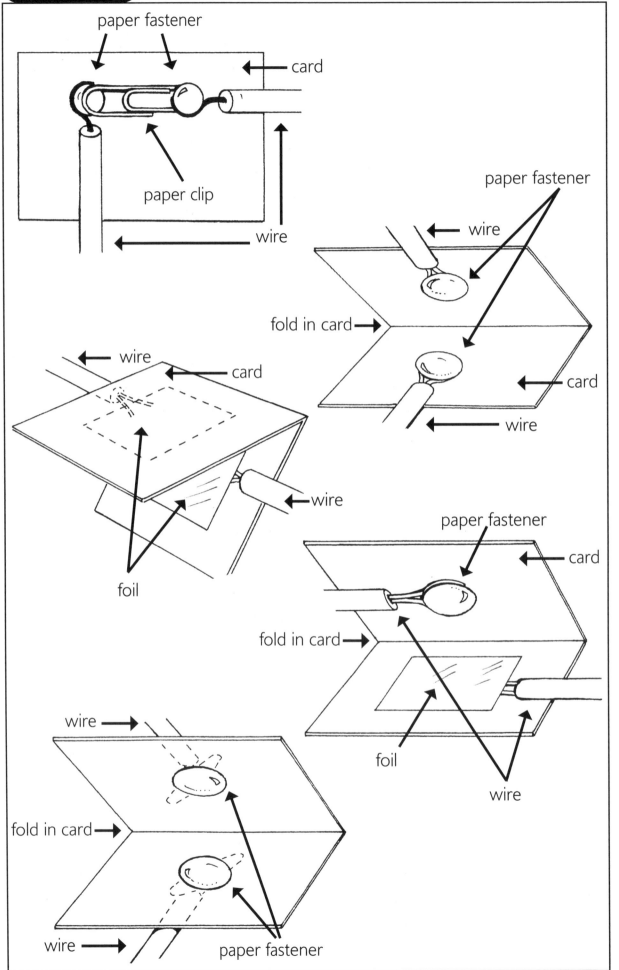

paper fastener

card

paper clip

wire

paper fastener

wire

fold in card

card

wire

wire

card

foil

paper fastener

card

fold in card

foil

wire

wire

fold in card

wire

wire

paper fastener

Illustration © Jane Bottomley

SCHOLASTIC PHOTOCOPIABLE

Design sheet

▲ Draw your design and label it with measurements, materials, how the circuit will be included and how the parts will be joined together.

▲ Who will use the light? _____

▲ What activity is your light for? _____

▲ To be successful it must:

1. _____

2. _____

3. _____

▲ Will you use a control technology program to control your light? If so, what will this do?

_____

_____

◀ SCHOLASTIC
PHOTOCOPIABLE

Planning sheet

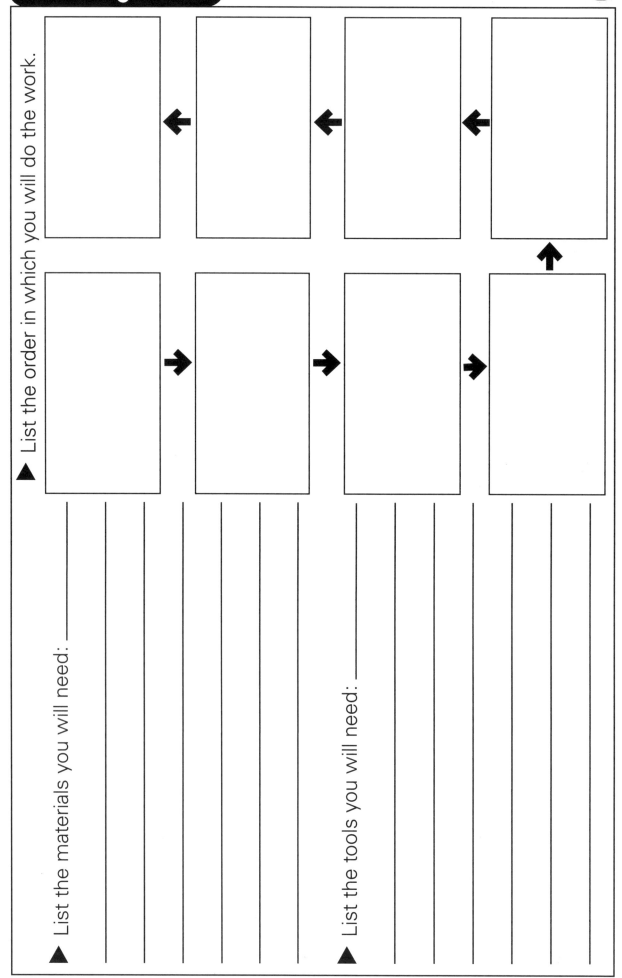

▲ List the order in which you will do the work.

▲ List the materials you will need: _____

▲ List the tools you will need: _____

■ SCHOLASTIC
PHOTOCOPIABLE

Evaluation sheet

▶ My light was designed to be used by: _____

▶ To be successful it had to:

1. _____ This worked well ☐ did not work well ☐

2. _____ This worked well ☐ did not work well ☐

3. _____ This worked well ☐ did not work well ☐

(Tick one box for each criterion.)

▶ Diagram or photograph of my finished light:

▶ My light could be improved by: _____

_____

_____

_____

_____

_____

📖 S C H O L A S T I C
P H O T O C O P I A B L E

SCHOLASTIC

Also available in this series:

ISBN 978-0439-98492-8

ISBN 978-0439-98493-5

ISBN 978-0439-98494-2

ISBN 978-0439-98495-9

ISBN 978-0439-98496-6

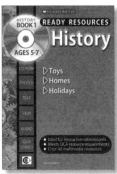

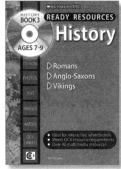

ISBN 978-0439-98497-9

ISBN 978-0590-53476-5

ISBN 978-0590-53477-2

ISBN 978-0439-98450-8

ISBN 978-0439-98451-5

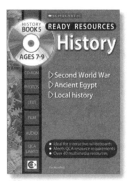

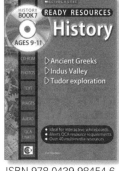

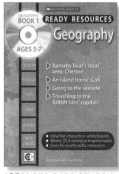

ISBN 978-0439-98452-2

ISBN 978-0439-98453-9

ISBN 978-0439-98454-6

ISBN 978-0439-98455-3

ISBN 978-0439-97193-5

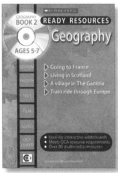
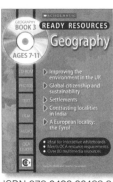
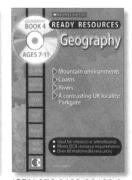

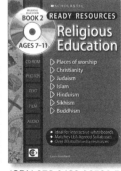

ISBN 978-0439-97194-2

ISBN 978-0439-96488-3

ISBN 978-0439-96489-0

ISBN 978-0439-96537-8

ISBN 978-0439-96538-5

ISBN 978-1407-10028-9

ISBN 978-1407-10029-6

ISBN 978-1407-10030-2

To find out more, call:
0845 603 9091

or visit our website
www.scholastic.co.uk